FIRST EDITION

AN INTRODUCTION TO WEB DEVELOPMENT

A CONCEPTUAL APPROACH

By Evelyn Stiller

Plymouth State University

cognella®
academic publishing

Bassim Hamadeh, CEO and Publisher
Michael Simpson, Vice President of Acquisitions
Jamie Giganti, Senior Managing Editor
Jess Busch, Senior Graphic Designer
John Remington, Senior Field Acquisitions Editor
Monika Dziamka, Project Editor
Brian Fahey, Licensing Specialist
Claire Yee, Interior Designer

www.cognella.com   800-200-3908

CONTENTS

CHAPTER THREE
HOW THE INTERNET WORKS   35

CHAPTER SEVEN
ANIMATION

CHAPTER ELEVEN
VIDEO   169

CHAPTER ONE

SETTING THE STAGE FOR WEB DEVELOPMENT

POINTS TO CONSIDER

- What distinguishes the Web from the Internet?
- What is Web 2.0?
- Why are blogs an important technology, and how can they enhance a democratic society?
- Give an example of how blogs have influenced the mainstream media.
- How do social media sites differ from regular websites?
- Why are privacy considerations so important for web developers?
- Which demographics might be excluded from web-based content?
- What material on the Web is restricted due to copyright?
- How can non-copyrighted material be produced, and why might one wish to do so?
- What elements comprise a web page/website, and how do these elements interrelate to each other?
- What is the purpose of an HTML file?

WHERE DID THE WEB COME FROM?

When Leonard Kleinrock sent the first message from his computer at the University of California, Los Angeles, to a computer at Stanford Research Institute over the first packet-switched network (Kleinrock 2010), he could not have foreseen where this technology would lead society in the coming decades. What connected these two computers would pave the way for what we understand to be the Web today. This communications network started out as a means for researchers to communicate and share data and other computer resources. During the late 1960s and early 1970s a series of networking protocols were developed for internetworking, that is, connecting multiple computer networks together. Advanced Research Projects Agency Network (ARPAnet) was the primary precursor to the Internet and connected mainly university and research facilities together. A standard set of protocols were developed in 1982,

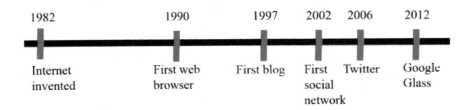

FIGURE 1.1 A chronological progression of major milestones for the Internet

which allowed computer networks around the world to communicate with each other (Kleinrock 2010). This global network became known as the Internet.

The event that transformed the Internet into the Web was the development in 1990 of the first web browser, initially named *World Wide Web,* but then renamed to *Nexus* to avoid confusion with the World Wide Web (Berners-Lee 2013). Web browsers, software that display multimedia content retrieved over the Internet, revolutionized the use of the Internet by supporting multimedia. Prior to this event, Internet tools displayed textual information only, so Nexus was the first Internet-based software to integrate text and images. Of course, modern web browsers support many additional multimedia file types, in addition to images. Today one can view a movie or listen to music using a wide array of web browsers, such as Firefox, Safari, Internet Explorer, or Chrome.

The next generation of the Web is defined by the ability of viewers of a website to supply content to that website without using complex tools or requiring special access to a web server. This new generation has been dubbed Web 2.0.

WEB 2.0—THE INTERACTIVE WEB

By the late 1990s, there was a tremendous amount of information available to anyone who had an Internet connection. This spurred speculation about a hyper-democratic society in which an entire population could be asked to express their opinions on numerous civic matters. However, a truly democratic technology would allow anyone to post information on the Internet, and through the late 1990s, one required significant training in technical matters, as well as access to a web server in order to express themselves publically over the Internet. This all changed with the advent of web logs, or blogs.

Blogs are a special form of web page that contains periodic chronological entries in a diary-like manner (Blood 2002). Blogs allow readers to leave comments on a particular blog entry, and a dialog can ensue if the blog author or others respond to comments. Another characteristic that distinguishes blogs from other web pages is that they are easy to create. Any person that has access to the Internet can create a blog free of charge using easy-to-use software. For the first time, Internet-based software allowed easy authorship of web content to the average, everyday person. This allowed individuals without the backing of a major media outlet to post information on the Web and, thereby, gain a following and influence public thinking.

An often cited example of the early influence of bloggers on public awareness occurred on the occasion of Strom Thurmond's 100th birthday in 2002. As Trent Lott, then Senate Majority Leader, praised Strom Thurmond's 1948 run for president as a Dixiecrat and, therefore, segregationist candidate, he suggested that the United States would have had fewer problems had Thurmond won the presidency. The major news outlets did not mention this racist comment when covering the birthday party, with the exception of ABC news (Scott and Jones 2004). Despite the initial lack of attention given this incident, bloggers expressed outrage. The furor grew amongst bloggers until the major networks could no longer suppress the story, and it became a major news item, leading to Trent Lott's resignation as Senate Majority Leader.

The next great revolution in the growth of web content was marked by the introduction of social networking sites starting in 2002. What defines this generation of web services is the ability to define one's own semi-private web universe using lists of contacts, referred to as *friends*. Though this type of technology was pioneered in 1997 by sites like SixDegrees (Boyd and Ellison 2007), its popularity exploded with the introduction of sites like Friendster, MySpace, LinkedIn, and Facebook. The advent of social media marks a new era of web software in which content is accessible by invitation only, as illustrated in Figure 1.2. Individuals may alter access to their social media content by changing privacy settings, but the default settings often restrict access to web content to those explicitly permitted. Another characteristic of certain social media sites is that the selected contacts (friends) of the owner of a site can be prompted whenever an update to the site takes place.

A more recent web-based innovation is micro-blogging in which users can send text-based messages of a maximum of 140 characters, in addition to multimedia content. Twitter was introduced in 2006 and is also classified as a social networking site, because registered members can subscribe to the messages or tweets of other users. Tweets are, by default, public but can be made available to subscribers only. There is one feature of Twitter that distinguishes it from other social media services. Public tweets can be searched and read by nonregistered users.

The next generation of Internet-based applications appears to be developing around wearable Internet devices, like Google Glass, which was unveiled in 2012 and became commercially available in 2014. Google Glass is worn like a pair of glasses and contains a video camera, allowing the wearer of the device to stream live video to the Internet. Google Glass functions as a full-fledged computer, running applications like Gmail,

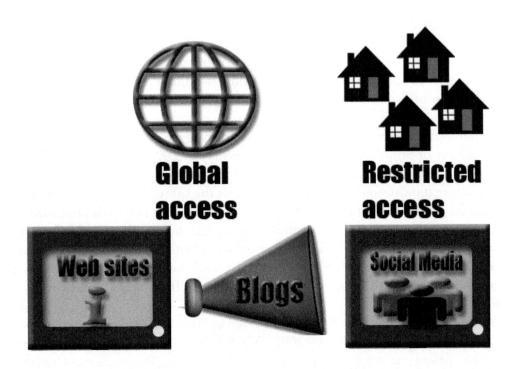

FIGURE 1.2 As web technology evolves, access has become more restricted.

Google Maps, and Google+. Wearers can interact with the device using voice commands or a touchpad. There are significant privacy concerns with this technology, because individuals may be recorded by wearers of the device without their knowledge or permission.

SOCIAL AND ETHICAL CONSIDERATIONS OF THE INTERNET

As the use of the Internet has evolved, more information, goods, and services have become web-based. So many people have grown accustomed to transacting business and finding information over the Web that organizations regard having a web-based presence as critical to their competitive edge. Having a multitude of goods, services, and information available over the Web is a great convenience for many people who have a computer and high-speed Internet access. It is important to understand that not everyone has such access, and we should ensure that participating fully in society does not exclude those who do not have Internet access.

Issues that can limit access to web-based services are numerous. The most obvious obstacle is the cost of maintaining a high-speed Internet connection required to access the multimedia content used in most websites. Many other circumstances may prohibit people from accessing web resources. For example, people may have physical or learning disabilities that prevent them from reading web content. Although the Americans with Disabilities Act requires that all websites accommodate people with disabilities, not all websites do. Another problem for many individuals, especially the elderly, is not being computer literate and/or lacking the manual dexterity to reliably move a computer cursor. Having taught older adults basic computer concepts, the author of this text has experienced firsthand how difficult it is for elderly individuals to learn to maneuver a computer mouse.

An important case-in-point involves the Medicare Part D benefit. Medicare is the government healthcare program for adults 65 and older, and Part D is the newly added drug benefit. As previously discussed, older adults are the least likely age group to use computers regularly, and while registration for the benefit can occur over the phone or by filling out a paper form, the information critical to determining the most beneficial drug plan for a given individual was only available online. We should ensure that the lack of Internet access does not create a group of people who cannot participate in important elements of society or are disadvantaged in some important way.

The many free web-based services are all tempting, but we pay a price for them, even if not monetarily. For example, the photos and text that Facebook account holders post belong to Facebook, and it has shared this information with the U.S. government and with other commercial organizations (Miller 2013). Facebook has had a history of changing privacy settings for individual accounts (Subramanian 2013), outraging its account-holders at various times. Facebook currently (at the writing of this book) has a privacy policy of aggregating information about individual account-holders from other Facebook accounts to supplement profile information. Figure 1.3 resembles graffiti seen in Germany that makes a connection between George Orwell's book, 1984, and Mark Zuckerberg,

FIGURE 1.3 Recreation of German graffiti

the founder of Facebook. This suggests that certain Germans feel that their privacy is being infringed upon by Facebook.

Another violator of account-holder privacy is Google. Google analyzes the content of emails sent from Gmail accounts to formulate client-specific advertisements (Fox 2004). For example, if someone mentions that they are traveling to Chicago, this person may get adds for hotels in that city. Our online behavior influences ads that appear under other circumstances, as well. If one searches for a golf course location using Google's web search, ads for golf-related items are likely to appear upon visiting other commercial websites.

As we create content on the Web, even in situations where we feel we have control over who has access to this information, we should consider a scenario where that changes. These changes to access may not only be a result of the corporation owning our data changing privacy settings or policy; for example, a prospective employer may require access to your Facebook account before considering you for a job. This is currently legal, so before posting something on your Facebook page, you may wish to consider what a future employer might think of this content.

Now that we have a sense of the services that make up the Web, we can move toward creating our own web-based contributions. We will explore the mechanics of getting

FIGURE 1.4 A sample web page to illustrate resource downloading

National Institutes of Health / Public Domain.

resources from the Web and the legal issues associated with this intellectual property as the next step before creating our own web content.

GETTING RESOURCES FROM THE WEB

Web pages contain a treasure trove of resources. We need to understand how to get available web resources, so that we can have building blocks for our websites. This section will also address what is available to us for use on our websites versus what is restricted. First, we'll discuss acquiring certain basic web elements.

Figure 1.4 shows a web page that contains typical multimedia resources, mostly consisting of formatted text and images. Other media types, like video and sound, are also common, but we will focus on downloading images first. Images can be inserted into a web page in a number of different ways. If an image is dynamically added to a web page using software like JavaScript or Adobe Flash, you may not be able to download the image. If the image is statically part of a web page, you can generally download this image by right-clicking on the image to reveal a menu similar to the one shown in Figure 1.5. The specific list of menu options will vary depending on which web browser you use, but you should find "Save image as" and "Copy image" in the list, if the image is downloadable.

There are many sources of multimedia content available, such as image searches using search engines, like Google, or media repositories, like Wikimedia or Opsound. There is good news and bad news concerning this easily available content. The bad news is that, by default, all content on the Internet is copyrighted and, therefore, off-limits for use. The good news is that many individuals are willing to share their content and have taken steps to allow others to use this content. As a result there is a large volume of

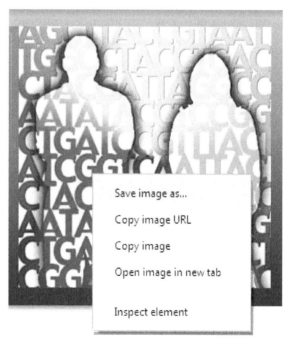

FIGURE 1.5 This Chrome menu appears after right-clicking on image.

National Institutes of Health / Public Domain.

non-copyrighted material available. The next section clarifies intellectual property considerations with typical web content.

INTELLECTUAL PROPERTY AND WEB RESOURCES

Intellectual property is a term that addresses a wide range of artifacts that embody original thought. Examples of intellectual property include music, songs, prose, poetry, non-fiction writing, design specifications for a new mouse trap, images, photographs, plays, computer software, choreography, movies, animations, and videos. Intellectual property laws are a means for society to protect individuals who produce such original works to encourage such efforts. Laws that protect intellectual property are copyrights, patents, trademarks, and laws addressing trade secrets and industrial design. Patentable material takes the form of an original idea, like an invention, whereas copyrightable material is some form of work. Examples of copyrightable works are books, poems, songs, lyrics, computer programs, photographs, paintings, sculptures, scripts, narrative texts, and so on. Rather than going into great detail about the categories of intellectual property, some of which are not common on the Internet, the focus will be on those works more commonly available online. Generally speaking, copyrighted material is what one is most likely to encounter on the web, so we will explore this law.

In the United States, copyright law is specified in Title 17 in the United States Code. The law specifies what the authors of a work are entitled to do with their works. The copyright holder may:

1. reproduce the work;
2. prepare derivative works;
3. distribute copies of the work to the public;
4. transfer copyright to a second party;
5. perform the work publicly and
6. display the work publicly.

The above rights imply that if we are *not* the copyright holder, we do not have the above rights.

Copyright is conferred upon the work immediately when it is created. The author does not need to register the work to receive protection. Because of this, *everything* that you encounter on the web is copyright-protected, unless the author explicitly indicates otherwise.

Fair Use

Even if a work is copyrighted, some use of the work can be legal. The term *fair use* addresses the legal use of copyrighted material. Factors influencing the determination of the use of a work as being fair are the amount of the work used, the purpose and manner of the use, and the effect of the use on the potential market for the work. For example, educational use is considered fair use, but an educator should not distribute copies of a textbook to his or her students, because that would diminish the market for the book. An educator could project a portion of the text on a screen in the classroom for discussion, however. Another example of fair use is use for criticism or parody. Small excerpts can be quoted to help clarify a critique of a work, or a small portion can be quoted or altered for the purpose of parody. Unless the use is for criticism or parody, copyrighted material cannot be posted to the web (unless we hold the copyright), because the web is a means to distribute material to the public.

Public Domain

Works in the public domain may be freely used, distributed, altered, copied, and sold. Examples of public domain works include the Declaration of Independence; works by Charles Dickens, Shakespeare, and Mozart; and the Linux operating system. Works are part of the public domain for a number of reasons. Copyright protection expires for works created after January 1, 1978, or seventy years after the creator's death. These works are then part of the public domain. Individuals may also elect to specify that their works can be freely used and are, therefore, part of the public domain. Finally, works of the U.S. Government are part of the public domain, because these works are publically funded.

Works under copyright protection allow those without rights little access, while works in the public domain offer limitless access. Fortunately, there are other options available to the authors of creative works who may find these two options too extreme. Developers of ideas may opt to associate a Creative Commons license with their works. We will explore this option next.

CREATIVE COMMONS

Creative Commons is an organization that started a movement to allow people to retain certain control of their work, but still allow their work to be used by others. The idea behind Creative Commons licenses is that society benefits from the free flow of creative ideas, but the author of a work should not have to relinquish all control or credit in order to disseminate his or her work.

Creative Commons defines a variety of usage options that the author may select when creating a Creative Commons license. The author responds to the following questions.

1. Can others modify your work?
2. If you permit modification of your work, must the derivative works also be shared?
3. Can others use your work in some way to make a profit?
4. What attribution information do you wish to have?

Creative Commons uses the responses to the above questions to create a custom license for the work. Figure 1.6 shows an example of such a license. The restriction on use in this example is that the person using the image must share the derived product with others and that the photographer must be credited.

When one adds the licensing options provided by Creative Commons to copyright and public domain options, there is a useful spectrum of licensing options that one may consider.

FIGURE 1.6 Sample Creative Commons license

Please keep these options in mind as you mine the Web for resources and create your own resources for your website.

There is one more essential topic to discuss before launching your first website, namely how to effectively store resources for your website.

WEBSITES: A COLLECTION OF FILES

A website consists of a collection of different files and file types, so it is important that we are mindful about where we save our files. It is also important to be aware of the file types that we are working with. A computer file is a name-accessible collection of information. For example, a file name might be *GrandCanyon.html*. The portion of the file name after the dot is called the *file extension* and can be used to determine the file type. Its file type is HTML, which we deduce from the file name. Some common file types with their associated file extensions are shown in Table 1.1.

In order to create a web page, the basic building block for a website, one needs an HTML file. For an HTML file to be the basis of a web page, it must be stored in a web-accessible directory or folder. A web-accessible folder resides on a web server, a special computer that allows connections over the Internet and responds to information requests over those connections. Most people work on computers that are not setup as web servers, so we need to transmit the files from our computer to the web server in order for our web page to be web-accessible. Figure 1.7 illustrates this scenario. In this figure the *local computer* represents the computer you have direct access to. You will probably develop all of your web resources on this computer and then upload them to a web server.

TABLE 1.1 File types and associated file extensions

FILE TYPE	FILE EXTENSION(S)	EXPLANATION
HTML	html, htm	Used to define a web page. Contains layout and formatting information, references to multimedia files, and hyperlinks.
Image file	jpg, png, gif	These are three common image file formats used on the web.
Cascading Style Sheet	css	Contains formatting information for web page content.
Sound file	wav, mpg3, wma	These are just a few common sound file formats.
Video file	mov, mpg4, wmv	These are just a few common video file formats.
Other resources	pdf, docx, xlsx, pptx, etc.	Other file types can be downloaded over the web and either opened using the web browser or using software on the local machine.

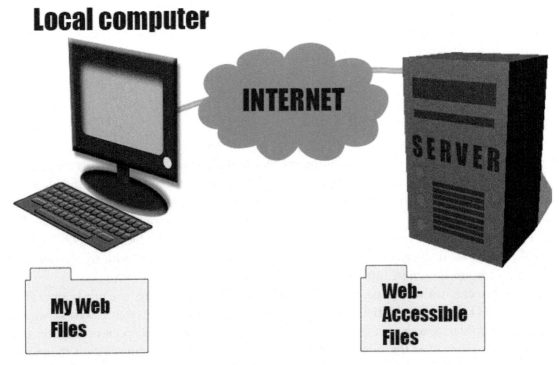

FIGURE 1.7 A common web development scenario

Organizing Your Files

It is extremely important to be organized and mindful as you develop your web content, so that you do not lose track of your files. If you are fortunate enough to have direct access to web-accessible folders, you will not need to worry about transferring your files to the web server. This brief discussion of file management will presume that you are creating your web content on a computer that is not accessible by others over the Internet to retrieve web content. In other words, your computer is not a web server.

Computers have permanent storage (files stored remain after the computer has been powered off) where one can store the files that will be the building blocks of a website. Depending on which operating system one uses, there may be predefined folders for storing certain types of information. For example, Microsoft's Windows 7 operating system predefines *Documents, Pictures, Music,* and *Video* folders. Generally speaking, when one creates a website, the files comprising the website need to be stored together within the same folder. Of course, if you are planning to create a very large website, or multiple websites, you may create additional folders within the umbrella web-accessible folder to better organize your web content.

Figure 1.8 illustrates a typical storage scenario on a local computer. In this scenario, the website content is stored in a folder called *public_html*. This folder name is the same as the name of the web-accessible folder on the server machine. On the local machine, you may name your organizing folder anything you wish. The name could be *myWebFiles* instead, for example. The scenario in Figure 1.8 suggests that there are two websites being developed. The specific files comprising each website are not shown in this first illustration.

An even simpler scenario for creating a website consisting of a single webpage containing four images is shown in Figure 1.9. The public_html folder could reside on the local machine or server machine. Many web servers use this name for the web accessible folder, but this name may differ depending on how the server is set up. It is important to keep in mind the basic principles of web content when managing your files. If something is to be visible on your website, you must have the file stored in the web-accessible folder or a folder contained inside the web-accessible folder. For example, when adding images to a web page, you must include the file for the web page, represented as *index.html* in the figure, as well as each image file, shown as *GrandCanyonView1.jpg* through *GrandCanyonView4.jpg*, in the figure. It is important to keep in mind that HTML files contain formatting information and references to multimedia files, like images, video, and sound, rather than embedding the multimedia in

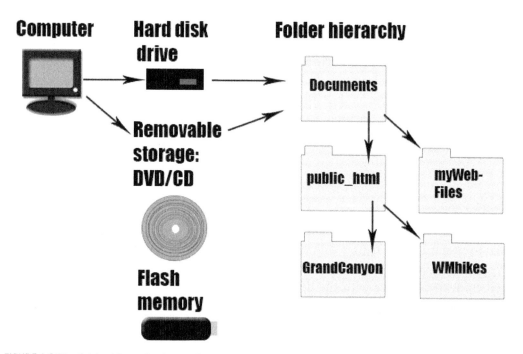

FIGURE 1.8 The folder hierarchy for storing your web content

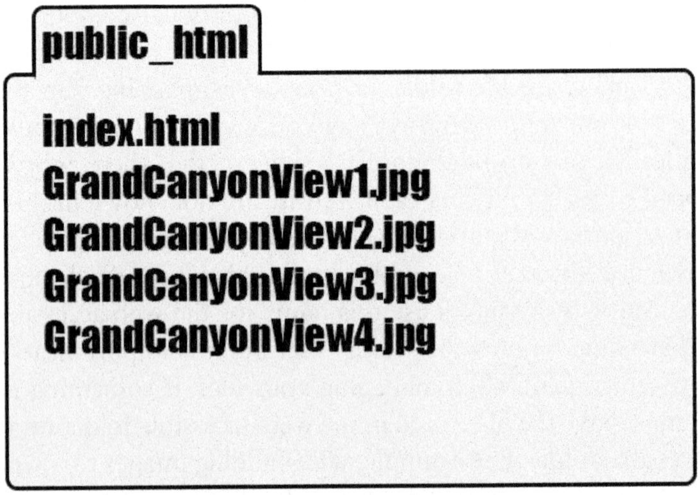

public_html

index.html
GrandCanyonView1.jpg
GrandCanyonView2.jpg
GrandCanyonView3.jpg
GrandCanyonView4.jpg

FIGURE 1.9 A very simple illustration of the files associated with a web page

the HTML file. This means that all files must reside in the web-accessible folder to be seen over the Web.

As we embark on creating our first web page, it merits repetition to be mindful about where (which device and folder) we save our files. Looking back at Figure 1.8, the removable storage devices, like the CD/DVD and flash memory, are important as backup media. We should frequently store on such a media an up-to-date version of our website in the event our computer crashes or some other circumstance should require retrieving our website files. The final reminder is that all content, including images, animations, videos, and sounds, must be stored in the web-accessible folder. Now it's time to create our first web page. Chapter 2 will guide us through this process.

SUMMARY

In order to prepare for our first web development experience, it is important to gain perspective on where our efforts fit in the context of the evolution of the Internet. The Web emerged from the Internet with the development of the first web browser in 1990. Since then, web-based technologies have exploded with the advent of web-logs, or blogs, and a host of social media sites. The current phase in technological evolution entails wearable technology. These recent web-based technologies facilitate the distribution of enormous amounts of personal information. Privacy considerations need to be in the forefront of everyone's mind as they contribute content to the web, even if the intended target is a small circle of friends. This concern emanates from possible unforeseen use of this information by the corporation that owns the social networking site. A final point to keep in mind in our web development efforts is that not everyone has equal access to content on the Internet. So, the audience for our website may omit important demographics.

With the wealth of easy-to-download content at our fingertips, it is particularly important to keep in mind that, unless otherwise indicated, all content is, by default, strictly owned by the author of the work. Fortunately, there are other options available beyond maintaining complete control of a work. One may relinquish all rights over a work by making it public domain. Should one wish to maintain certain ownership rights, Creative Commons may be used to create a custom license. As a result of these options, a great deal of content is available on the web that has been shared in some way.

When developing our websites, we should keep in mind that each website is a collection of interrelated files. The text, format and color of each page are defined in the HTML files. These HTML files also contain references to multimedia files, like images, video, and sound files, so it is important that these files are all located in a web-accessible folder on a web server.

REFERENCES

Berners-Lee, T. The WorldWideWeb browser. Retrieved June 24, 2013 from http://www.w3.org/People/Berners-Lee/WorldWideWeb.html.

Blood, R. (2002). *The Weblog Handbook: Practical Advice on Creating and Maintaining your Blog.* Cambridge, MA, Perseus Publishing.

Boyd, D. M., & Ellison, N. B. (2007). Social Network Sites: Definition, History, and Scholarship. *Journal Of Computer-Mediated Communication*, 13(1), 210–230.

Fox, S. (2004). Privacy Fears Dog Google's Free E-Mail. *PC World*, 22(7), 49.

Kleinrock, L. (2010, June 7). Personal History/Biography: the Birth of the Internet. Retrieved June 28, 2013 from http://www.lk.cs.ucla.edu/personal_history.html.

Miller, Claire Cain (2013, June 7). "Tech Companies, Bristling, Concede to Federal Surveillance Program", *New York Times*, p B1.

Scott, E. & Jones, A. (2004, Feb. 1). "Big Media" Meets the "Bloggers": Coverage of Trent Lott's Remarks at Strom Thurmond's Birthday Party, Harvard Business Publishing. (report #C14-04-1731.0) Retrieved June 30, 2013 from https://www.case.hks.harvard.edu/caseTitle.asp?caseNo=1731.0.

Subramanian, C. (2013). Facebook No Longer Lets Users Hide Their Profiles in Search Box. *Time.Com*, 1.

CHAPTER TWO

CREATING YOUR FIRST WEB PAGE

POINTS TO CONSIDER

- What options exist for creating/editing web pages?
- How is it possible to use a text editor to create a web page?
- What is WYSIWYG software?
- What is open source software?
- What is proprietary software?
- What is source code?
- What is binary/object code?
- What is an operating system?
- Give an example of an operating system.
- What is the World Wide Web Consortium?
- Why is Amaya a desirable web page development tool?
- What are good web page development practices?
- What types of content should one avoid putting on the web?
- (optional) Where can one find information about creating HTML instructions?

INTRODUCTION

In the previous chapter, a website was described as a collection of files of various types. The file types comprising a website are HTML (Hypertext Markup Language) and other multimedia types, like images, sound, and video, although other types of files are also possible. Although other considerations are critical to creating an effective website, like the design and analysis of content, one can view the process of creating a website, at its simplest, as creating the files that comprise each web page. So, in this chapter, we will focus on the mechanics of creating a web page, rather than emphasizing design. The first web page we will create will contain some formatted text and an image. Design considerations will be discussed in chapter six.

SELECTING YOUR SOFTWARE

An important set of decisions one must make is to determine what software to use when developing web content. The first piece of software necessary allows us to format web pages and add text and multimedia content. A significant philosophical choice that has been made in this text is to rely primarily on WYSIWYG software for web page creation. WYSIWYG is an acronym that stands for "what you see is what you get." This implies that web pages will be created using software that has a graphic interface that hides the HTML comprising the web page. That is, we will not use a text editor to compose HTML directly, but let the software generate the HTML for us.

Because there are times when our software fails to do exactly what we need it to do, there is an optional section on basic HTML at the end of this chapter. Most WYSIWYG web page creation software allows individuals to view and edit HTML directly, so it is useful to have a basic fluency in HTML.

There are many choices when it comes to selecting web page creation software, but if one wants maximum flexibility for web content and design and wishes to retain exclusive ownership rights for the content, then the options are fewer. If you do not mind having limited design choices and having your web content hosted and owned by another company, like Google, then there are many choices one can make. This text will not explore these options, but rather discuss two specific options not associated with a web-hosting site.

The two options for web page development discussed here are Amaya and Adobe Dreamweaver. Amaya is freely available and is distributed by the World Wide Web Consortium (W3C) the organization that oversees standards and protocols for the Web. Adobe Dreamweaver is a commercial product that many professional web developers use. When specific examples are given in the text, Amaya will be used to illustrate the example, but there will be helpful examples and information available at the textbook website to support web development using Adobe's software, as well.

The advantage of using W3C's Amaya is that it is a free product and will continue to evolve with developing Web standards, since it is produced by the organization in charge of those standards. However, free software can be harder to learn than some commercial products, because market pressures often motivate corporations to be more sensitive to customer needs. We will use Amaya in this text, because it is easily available to anyone who wishes to use it and is reasonably easy to use.

INTRODUCTION TO AMAYA

Amaya is a freely available, *open source* web page editing tool. The term open source indicates that the distributor of the software not only provides the *executable* version of the software, but also distributes the *source code*. Executable code, also referred to as *binary* or *object code*, runs directly on a computer after installation. Source code is the basis for the executable version and allows customization of the software. Those who customize the software may elect to share their improvements with others, thus creating a community of software developers for that product. In contrast, Adobe Dreamweaver, a commercial web page editing tool, is referred to as *proprietary* software. The manufacturer only distributes the executable version, to protect its trade secrets, which are embedded in the software. This approach gives the corporation exclusive control over the software.

Downloading Amaya

You may download the executable/binary version of Amaya at: http://www.w3.org/Amaya/User/BinDist.html. At the Amaya software download website, look for the *operating system* that you are running on your computer to determine which version to download. The operating system is the software that you interact with when you are not running another application, like a word processor, web browser, image editor, music player, and so on. The operating system serves as the interface between you and the computer. Examples of operating systems are, Microsoft Windows, MacOS, and Linux.

After selecting the desired version of Amaya, you might be prompted to either run/open or save the file for installation. If this is the case, run/open would be the easiest option. If you download the file, it is important you can find the file in order to begin the installation process. Some web browsers have a standard folder where downloaded files are stored, while others allow you to determine where the file is stored. If you do not know the location of your file, you can search for your file. In Microsoft Windows the search option is available after clicking on the Window's start icon at the lower left corner of your computer screen.

If you are a novice at installing software on your computer, it is important to read each prompt or question that arises during the installation process. Generally speaking, it is safe to select the *default value*, which is the suggested value that is used unless overridden with another desired value. Once the installation process is complete, you are ready to start your first web page. This text will provide introductory information to help you get started.

Approach to How-to Information in this Text

This text provides introductory and background information for first-time web developers on basic web-development activities, like web page editing and formatting, image editing, sound editing, basic video creation and editing, and animation. There is a wealth of up-to-date how-to information available on the Internet, so this text provides some initial how-to information so that individuals can get started, and then directs readers to other sources of information to learn more. With this philosophy in mind, we are ready to create our first web page.

CREATING YOUR FIRST WEB PAGE

The Amaya Interface

When you first start Amaya, you will see a welcome screen and a dialog box containing some hints to help you learn how to use Amaya. Figure 2.1 shows the basic Amaya interface with the default web page. There are four main sections to note on the Amaya interface, as illustrated by Figure 2.2. The first section of the Amaya interface illustrated in the figure is

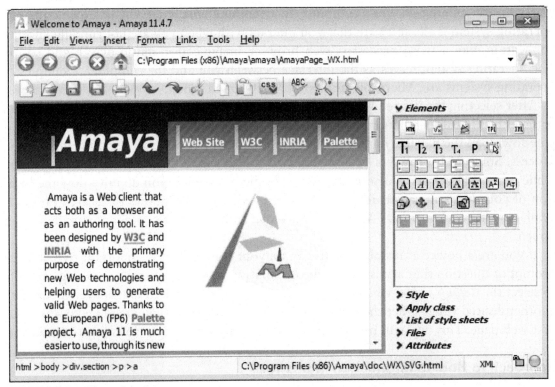

FIGURE 2.1 The Amaya interface

Source: W3C / INRIA.

Main menu bar

Web browser navigation icons

Icons for common functions

Icon/form driven commands

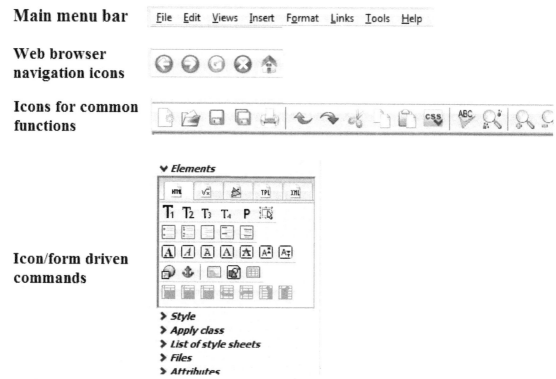

FIGURE 2.2 Important sections of the Amaya interface

Source: W3C / INRIA.

the main menu bar. Each menu item in the main menu expands to a list of options when clicked upon, as shown in Figure 2.3. The main menu bar is particularly important because it will be the basis of all how-to information provided in this text.

The other three sections of the Amaya interface provide either web browser commands or icon-driven alternatives to the main menu bar. Figure 2.1 shows the web browser navigation icons, which are important when one uses Amaya in its capacity as a web browser. The five icons in the web browser control section represent in sequence from left to right, *next page, previous page, reload page, cancel,* and *go to the home page,* respectively. The next two sections in the Amaya interface are convenient for web page editing, and they cover the same functions as the main menu. We will not refer to the icon driven areas during the how-to explanations, because specifying a sequence of menu options can be done more clearly and unambiguously than describing which icon to use.

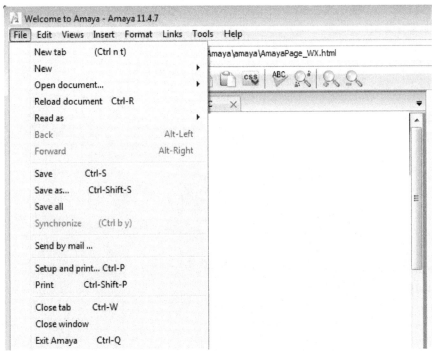

FIGURE 2.3 Expanding the menu item "File"

Source: W3C / INRIA.

Good Practices

This section serves as a brief reiteration of some good practices discussed in chapter one. When developing content for your web page, make sure you do the following:

1. be mindful of where (which folder) you store the files you create for your website;
2. keep in mind that all content you create for your website must be moved/stored to a web accessible folder on the web server, so it is a good idea to store your files in the same folder (subfolders under a main folder is fine);
3. as you work on your website content, save your files early and often, and
4. backup your files on another storage medium, like flash memory stick, CD or DVD.

Elements of the First Web Page

In order to keep our first web development objectives as simple as possible, we will select a simple goal for our first web page. We will create a web page about our favorite hobby or travel experience. This page could serve as a building block for a website, if we wish to continue to develop web content on this theme. Figure 2.4 shows a sample web page that

FIGURE 2.4 Goal for the web development exercise

we will use to illustrate our web page development process. Our goal for this web page creation exercise is to is to gain experience in the following web page definition tasks:

1. change the background color for the page;
2. add a heading;
3. add text;
4. change the color, font and alignment of the text;
5. add an image;
6. add a link to an external website.

How to Create Your First Web Page

1. Start Amaya
2. Create a new web page (called *document* in Amaya). Click on the main menu options *File → New → New document*. Note that the arrows indicate a sequence of menu selections.
3. The dialog box shown in Figure 2.5 should pop up after you carry out the above step. This is the time to be mindful about where to store your files. Use the folder icon,

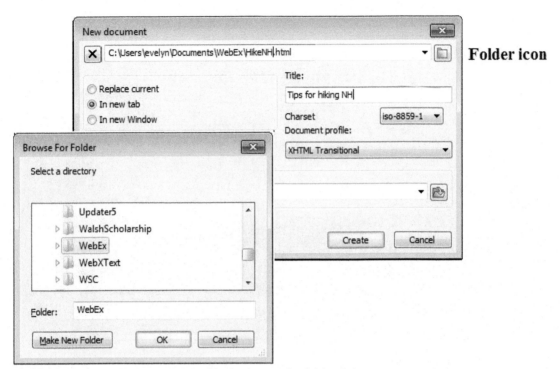 **Folder icon**

FIGURE 2.5 The *new document* dialog with the *browse for folder* dialog

Source: W3C / INRIA.

shown in Figure 2.5, to navigate to and create a folder for your web content. Also, give your web page a title using the same dialog box. You now have a web page, but it consists of a swath of white.

4. <u>Change the background color of the web page</u> (document) to a pleasant and not-too-dark earth tone, or other color suitable to the content you are creating. In order to do this, we need to indicate that we want the *entire* web page to have the specified background color. Other elements of the web page, like a section of text, could also have a separate background color. Amaya indicates which component of our web page is the focus for editing in the lower left-hand corner of the screen. Figure 2.6 shows an Amaya screen in which the lower left corner shows *html > body > Element*. In order to apply the background color to the entire page, we need to select *html*. You can do this by <u>pressing the F2 key twice</u>. This will cause the lower left corner of the Amaya window to read *html*. This means that when you change the background color, it will be applied to the entire page. Now, select the main menu items *Format → Background color → Select a background color ...* Next, use the color picker dialog box to select a desired color. You will probably want to define a custom color for this rather than selecting

one of the predefined colors. Please note that in Amaya the web page does not seem to be fully colored in the background color, but if you save your web page and open it in another web browser, like Firefox or Safari, you will see that the entire page is in this color.

5. Add a heading for your web page by selecting the main menu items *Insert* → *Heading* → *T1 h1*, as shown in Figure 2.7. The letters *h1* are the HTML code for the largest heading, while the *T1* is used to illustrate relative text sizes. The letters shown in the parentheses are the shortcut for the command.

6. Change the color of the heading by selecting the heading. The heading can be selected by dragging the mouse over it, causing a blue background to appear over a white heading, as

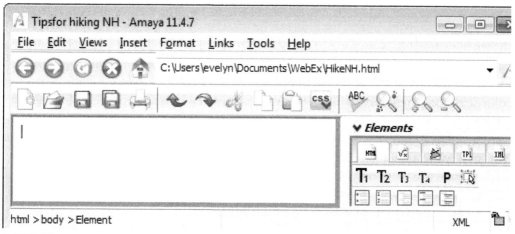

FIGURE 2.6 The lower left corner of the screen shows which component is selected for editing

Source: W3C / INRIA.

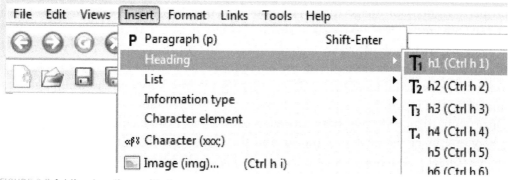

FIGURE 2.7 Adding headings with Amaya

Source: W3C / INRIA.

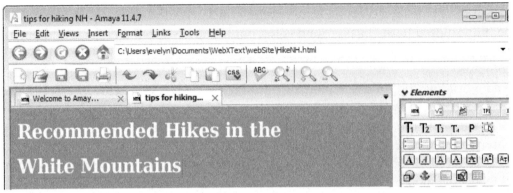

FIGURE 2.8 Selecting the heading to change colors and fonts

Source: W3C / INRIA.

shown in Figure 2.8. Now you are ready to select a color. If you have a lighter color for your background, then select a darker color for your heading for good readability. Select a color by clicking on the main menu items *Format → Text color → select a color*. Then use the color-selection dialog box to pick a suitable color. A dark green was selected for the sample web page.

7. Center the heading by selecting the main menu items *Format → Alignment → Center*.

8. You may wish to select a different font for the heading, as well. Keep in mind that when others are viewing your web page, they may not have a particular font installed on their web browser, so Amaya provides a very small selection of standard fonts. You may change the font of selected text by clicking on the main menu item *Format → Character → Select of font ...*

9. Save your HTML file in a web-accessible folder or a folder that you plan to copy to a web accessible folder. Save your file by selecting the main menu options *File → Save*.

10. <u>Insert an image</u>. You may select an image from the Internet (keeping in mind intellectual property rights), an image for which you hold the copyright, or the images provided at the website for this textbook website. Do not forget that the HTML file that you are editing with Amaya, as well as the image file, must be stored in a web-accessible folder. It may seem as though you are embedding the image in the HTML file, but you are linking to the image. Once you have set up the link between the web page and the image, do not move the image file relative to the HTML file.

11. Once your image file has been stored in a web-accessible folder, <u>place your cursor where you want the image to appear</u> and then select the main menu options *Insert → Image (Img) ...* A dialog box, like the one in Figure 2.9 should pop up and allow you to navigate to your image file. Also, use this dialog box to specify *alternate text*. Alternate text appears if the image does not download properly; a cursor hovers over the image,

FIGURE 2.9 Dialog box used for inserting images into a web page
Source: W3C / INRIA.

and it is used by screen readers, which are used by individuals needing assistance reading web pages.

12. <u>Center your image</u>. Click on your image to select it. Then select the main menu options *Format → Alignment → Center*.

13. Do not forget to save your HTML file often (*File → Save*).

14. Add some text after the image. Press the *enter* key once or twice to move the cursor under the image. Now type some text, such as "A great guide to hikes in the White Mountains: AMC WM Guide Online."

15. Change the text color. First, drag your cursor over the text to select it, and then select the main menu options *Format → Text color → Select a text color*. Use the color selection dialog box to find a color that has good contrast with the background color and that fits with the content.

16. Change the text size. First, drag your cursor over the text to select it, and then select the main menu options *Format → Character → Select a font*. Use the dialog box to select a larger font size, such as 14-point.

17. <u>Create a link to an external website</u>. Use a web browser of your choice and navigate to a website that you would like to link to. Select a portion of the text entered in the previous step that you want to serve as the link by dragging your mouse over it, and then select from the main menu *Links → Create or change link …* You should see a dialog box that allows you to enter a Uniform Resource Identifier (URI), as shown in Figure 2.10. Copy the web address from your web browser, which should start with *http://*, and paste this in the text field in the dialog box. Then press the confirm button. Your selected text should be underlined, indicating that it is a link.

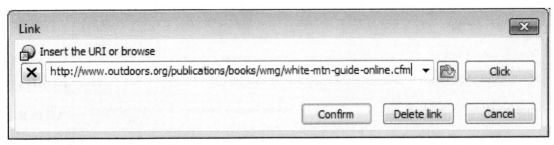

FIGURE 2.10 Dialog for creating a link

Source: W3C / INRIA.

18. <u>Save your web page (*File → Save*) and copy your image file and your html file to a web accessible folder</u> if it is not already there.
19. <u>Test your web page by using a web browser to navigate to it</u>. Type your URI into the address field of the web browser. You may need to ask your Internet Service Provider (ISP) or instructor to determine what your URI is. Test the link on your web page to ensure it works. If your image does not show up, make sure your image file is in the web accessible folder.
20. You may continue to work on your web page by adding text, images, and links. Don't forget to save your work often and test it.

BASIC INTRODUCTION TO HTML (OPTIONAL)

HTML is a computer language that allows us to define web pages. Fortunately, there are many computer applications that allow individuals to create web pages without having to formulate HTML instructions directly. On occasion it is useful to understand a bit of HTML, in the event the web page editing tool we are using does not function correctly. There are also times when certain web page editing tools make reference to HTML tags, like the bottom left corner of Amaya, as can be seen in Figure 2.12.

Amaya allows one to view the HTML instructions that comprise a web page. One can do this by using the main menu options *Views → Show source*. Figure 2.12 shows the result of revealing the source of the very simple web page illustrated in Figure 2.11

HTML allows the identification of a variety of types of elements that comprise a web page, like headings, text, images, links, sound, video, and so on. HTML uses *tags* to distinguish these different types of elements. Line 12 in Figure 2.11 shows the tag for the largest category of heading, *h1*. The characters, <h1>, indicate the beginning of the heading element, and </h1> indicates the end of this element. All tags are paired with a beginning

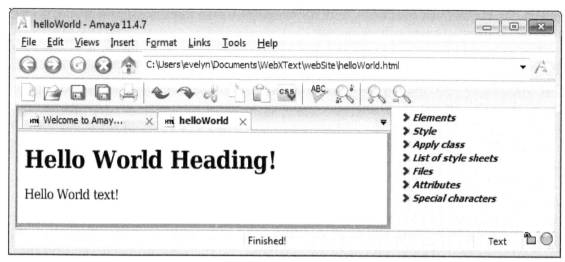

FIGURE 2.11 Very simple web page

Source: W3C / INRIA.

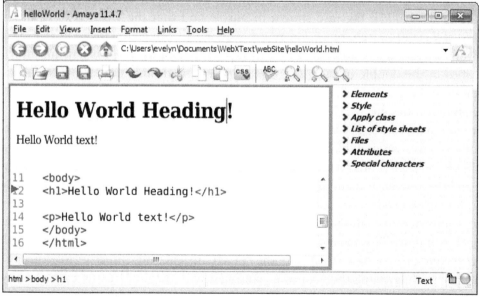

FIGURE 2.12 View of partial source of the simple web page

Source: W3C / INRIA.

and ending tag. Because the cursor is on the heading, Amaya indicates the element type, h1, at the bottom left corner of the window.

The *p* tag identifies regular text that does not serve as a heading. Line 14 in Figure 2.12 illustrates how this tag is used to create the second line of the simple web page. Also note that lines 11 and 15, the "begin body" and "end body" instructions, respectively. These instructions delimit the HTML used for adding content to our website. The instructions above the body of the web page (not shown in Figure 2.12) are part of the header, which includes style information and determines the title of the web page. The web page title appears in the upper left-hand corner of the web browser.

Both of the elements comprising our simple web page, the heading and text, are unformatted. That is, no color, font, or alignment information has been specified. The default color is black; the default alignment is left-justified; and the default font is Times New Roman. You can format the header or the text using the *Format* menu option. Figure 2.13 shows the result of changing the color of each element. Note the change in the HTML in lines 12 and 14, corresponding to the color change.

Note in the HTML in Figure 2.13 that the color information is contained inside the start header tag, <h1>. HTML tags are delimited by the less-than and greater-than signs, so if a portion of the instruction appears between these characters, it applies to the tag. So, line 12 applies the color *#8000ff,* to the header. HTML uses hexadecimal numbers to determine color information. How this works is explained in the chapter discussing images. You may note that all the HTML tags are shown in purple and that the word *style* is also purple. The word *style* is not a tag, but a *key word*. Key words are character sequences that have special significance in HTML. The key word, style, indicates that formatting information is contained in the double quotes. The text between the double quotes is yet another web page definition language, called *Cascading Style Sheets* or *CSS*. CSS will be touched upon in the chapter on design.

There are many other HTML tags and key words, such as <a> which stands for a link (web address), and <img> which stands for an image. This textbook is not intended to serve as an HTML reference, but rather to provide an introduction. Many HTML references exist online, and the reference maintained by the W3C is located here: http://docs.webplatform. org/wiki/html/elements.

A final consideration about HTML is that the language is written in plain text and the language is standard. This means that you can edit a web page using any web page editor or even a text editor (if you wish to specify the HTML instructions directly). So you can start a web page using Amaya and then continue editing it with Adobe Dreamweaver, or any other web page editor, without any problem. To better appreciate this flexibility, consider editing a word processing document written in MS Word. One cannot start a document in MS Word and then continue editing it using a text editor or other word processing software, unless the document goes through some form of conversion. HTML does not need any

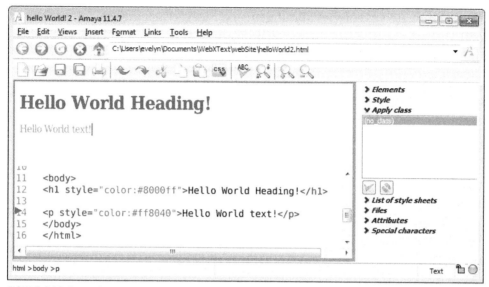

FIGURE 2.13 Changing the default colors in "Hello World"

Source: W3C / INRIA.

form of conversion if one chooses to edit a web page using different types of web page editing software.

NETIQUETTE AND PRIVACY CONSIDERATIONS

Now that we have covered introductory information on creating web pages, a few words are in order concerning their content. Generally speaking, the content of a website should reflect positively on its author and should treat others with respect. In addition, we should be aware of privacy concerns and how others might misuse information posted on our websites.

Be sure to reflect positively on yourself by following the standards listed below.

1. Correct any spelling errors by using spell check. Most web page editors have a spell check function available, including Amaya.
2. Use good grammar.
3. Check your facts. Do not post erroneous information.
4. If you have a conflict of interest or bias that pertains to the content on your website, let people know.

5. Do not perpetuate stereotypes about genders, races, ethnicities, religions, physical and mental abilities, body types, gender identification, and sexual preferences.
6. Do not include hate speech.

Be mindful of people's right to privacy. Web pages are accessible worldwide, and you should not disseminate information about individuals unless they are public figures. Contact information may be provided only to facilitate communication with individuals in their professional capacity, like fire chief, police chief, principal of a school, political representative, and so on. The information you should avoid using is,

1. names;
2. personal phone numbers;
3. non-work email addresses (including your own);
4. address of residence; or
5. images with unflattering portrayals.

A final consideration is that many organizations and individuals, some with ill intent, scour the Web for information. If you put your email address on your website in clear text, you are likely to be bombarded with spam. Spammers have programs that search web pages looking for email addresses. If you wish to communicate your email address to people viewing your website, but not to programs looking for data, you can embed your email address in an image, which is much more difficult for programs to read.

SUMMARY

Web sites are a collection of interrelated files that reside on a web server in a web-accessible folder. At the center of any website are HTML files with their associated media files, like images, sounds, videos and animations. HTML stands for Hypertext Markup Language, which is a computer language that allows the formatting of web pages. It is important to keep in mind that HTML files reference media files, but do not embed this content. This means that all files that make up a web page, including image files and other media files, (not just the HTML files) must be located in a web- accessible folder. Because HTML files are text files, they can be created or edited by any number of software applications, ranging from text editors to special purpose web page editing software. The advantage of using software designed for web page editing is that one can generally specify the format and contents of a web page in a WYSIWYG mode, and can thus avoiding specifying HTML commands directly. This textbook addresses website development using software that does not require an understanding of HTML. Choosing the right web page development software is important. Amaya is used in this textbook because of its reliability, quality, and lack of cost.

As we embark on developing our first web page, we should keep in mind our own privacy needs and the privacy rights of others. We should not include personal information of individuals who do not have celebrity status in our web pages. Our websites should also reflect our intelligence and maturity by avoiding factual inaccuracies, checking for and correcting spelling and grammar errors, and avoiding unflattering portrayals of ourselves. Finally, we should omit content that can be harvested by programs that search the Internet for private information like names, email addresses, residential addresses, and phone numbers.

HOW THE INTERNET WORKS

POINTS TO CONSIDER

- What distinguishes the Web from the Internet?
- What is a URL/URI?
- What elements comprise a URL/URI?
- What is the purpose of HTML?
- Do HTML files embed multimedia content?
- Where must a media file reside in order to appear on a web page?
- Name four web browsers. What is the purpose of a web browser?
- How do search engines work?
- What is a web crawler/spider?

- What role do databases play in web searching?
- Why are web searches so fast?
- What is meant by "filtering the Web"?
- How might two individuals get different results for the same web search?
- Why might filtering the web be harmful to a democratic society?
- What is web page metadata?
- What is Google's pageRank?
- What is a web page's suitability for a web search?
- What is meant by a modular design for a website?

HOW THE WEB WORKS

The use of the term Internet, as opposed to Web, in this text has a specific significance. As you may recall in chapter one, the history of the Web begins with the development of the Internet and later leads to the development of the Web. The Web is the Internet with multimedia support. This is accomplished through a layer of software, such as web browsers and web server software, that accepts requests for information over Internet connections. The computer language that allows web servers to accurately service information requests from individuals using web browsers is Hypertext Markup Language (HTML). HTML is the language we use directly or indirectly (through a web authoring tool like Amaya or Adobe Dreamweaver) when we create web pages. HTML allows people to specify how text and multimedia elements, like images, video, and sound, should be laid out. Hypertext Transfer Protocol (HTTP) is the protocol that the web browser uses to inform the web server of the web browser's information request. The web browser issues commands to a web server using the HTTP protocol and then interprets the .html files to correctly format each web page.

The Internet originally consisted of a network infrastructure that allowed for the exchange of information and remote access to computers. The Individual requesting information over the Internet uses a suite of software applications in which information requests are issued using text-based commands. Examples of Internet applications are Telnet, FTP, and Gopher. To a large extent, things have not changed radically. Much of what transpires between web servers and web browsers is rooted in text-based commands. What is different is that some of the files being exchanged contain HTML commands that instruct web browsers how to format multimedia content.

A concrete example can help clarify the nuts and bolts of how the web functions. Figure 3.1 starts this example, by illustrating what one might type into the address field of a web browser, like Internet Explorer, Chrome, Firefox, or Safari. Someone could type in

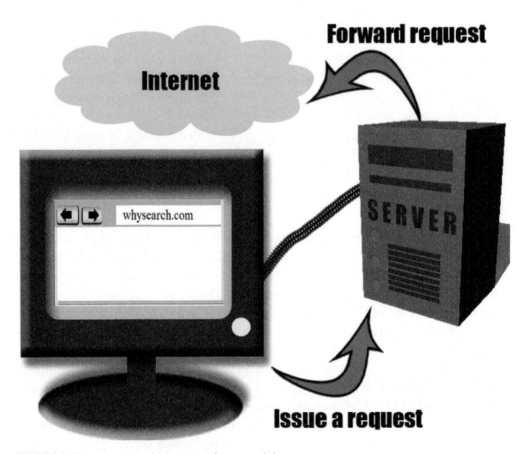

FIGURE 3.1 Illustrating a typical request from a web browser

"whysearch.com" to navigate to a fictitious search engine website. The web browser would interpret this web address as being part of the HTTP and reformat the address as: http:// www.whysearch.com.

The Uniform Resource Locator (URL), also known more generally as Uniform Resource Identifier (URI) http://www.whysearch.com consists of three elements. The protocol of the information request is identified by *http://*. The letters, *www*, indicate the resource is part of the World Wide Web, and the final portion of the address, *whysearch.com*, is called the *domain name*. The Internet is made up of special servers, called domain name system (DNS) servers that translate the domain name into a numeric Internet Protocol (IP) address. The numeric IP address allows for rapid location of the requested server with the requested web page. The information request is passed along from computer to computer until the web server at the specified IP address receives the request and sends the requested files to the computer originating the request.

The example in Figure 3.1, requesting the domain whysearch.com, does not appear to specify any files, and yet a web page is retrieved (or would be retrieved, if this website existed) in response. Web servers retrieve default files, typically *index.html*, in response to a request, if no file is specified. The web server then sends index.html to the requesting computer. The web browser interprets the HTML commands in the file to format the web page and possibly make additional requests for image, video, or sound files to complete the web page.

Another example illustrating a URL in which a file is specified as opposed to re-questing the default file is illustrated by *http://jupiter.plymouth.edu/~estiller/Fall2015/ WebExpressionsFall2015.html*. This URL indicates that the HTTP protocol will be ob-served for the information request. The web server is *jupiter* in the domain *plymouth. edu*. The character sequence, *~estiller* specifies an account on the web server. *Fall2015* is a directory in the web accessible folder for this account and *WebExpressionsFall2015.html* is the .html file, which identifies the content of the web page and how it should be formatted, including any other files that comprise this web page. Figure 3.2 shows that the domain *plymouth.edu* consists of a number of regular computers and three web server computers. On the server named *jupiter* there is an account for *estiller* with a web-accessible folder that contains a folder called *Fall2015*, which in turn contains the file *WebExpressionsFall2015. html*.

In the two preceding scenarios one domain name ended in *.com*, while the other ended in *.edu*. These domain name endings are called *generic top-level domains* and are regulated by the Internet Corp for Assigned Names and Numbers (ICANN). Many of the original domain name suffixes are probably familiar, com, edu, gov, mil, org, and .net. Additional suffixes have been introduced, bringing the total to around twenty-two, but the ICANN is currently in the process of expanding the suffixes to total more than 1,500 (Singer 2013). New endings

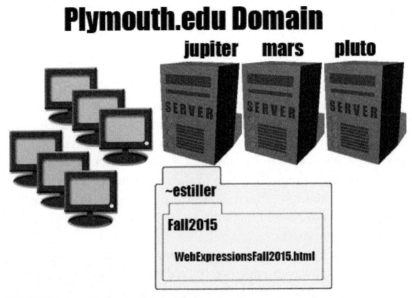

FIGURE 3.2 A hypothetical configuration for the Plymouth.edu domain

would include things like .hotel, .credit, and .blog, providing a clearer indication of the mission of the sought after website.

Entering a specific URL into a web browser is one way to get web content, but for much of our web access we do not know a specific location on the web that contains the information that we need. For these cases we need to use a search engine. We will explore how search engines work next.

HOW SEARCH ENGINES WORK

Search engines are websites that allow people to specify desired information. The search engine then returns a list of websites that contain the specified information. When one enters one or more search terms into the search field of a search engine like Google, Yahoo, or Bing, it is quite incredible that results are returned in a fraction of a second. The volume of information that resides on the Internet is mind boggling. As of August 2013, NetCraft, an Internet research and security company, detected over 700,000,000 responsive websites on the Internet and is expecting the Internet to reach the billion mark by the early part of 2015 (NetCraft 2013). How search engines return results so quickly despite the large volume of information and vast number of servers to consult merits explanation.

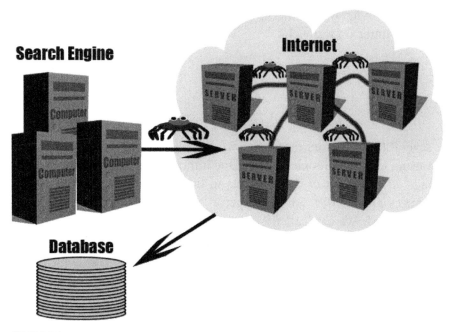

FIGURE 3.3 Illustrating a search engine using web crawlers to process the Internet

The reason search engines return results so quickly is because they process the contents of the Web with their own computers and build a *database* of topics before you enter your search terms. A database is a sophisticated repository of information that facilitates quick information retrieval. Figure 3.3 illustrates a search engine using multiple computers to initiate programs that connect to all accessible websites and process information at each site. These programs are often called *web crawlers* or *spiders* because they maneuver from web server to web server parsing each website. The web crawlers/spiders return their results to the search engine computers which then update a database for quick information retrieval when individuals enter search terms into the search engine website.

When someone enters a search term using a search engine, the database is searched to create the results page. A database entry pairs website contents with web addresses, so when the searched-for information is located in the database, the web address where it can be found is immediately available. For example, if one wanted to investigate hiking opportunities in the White Mountains, the terms, *hiking* and *White Mountains* could be entered into a search engine. In this case over seven hundred thousand results are returned in a quarter of a second. With so many results, one may wonder how the search engine determines which result to return first. How search engines prioritize their results can be an important reason to select one search engine over another. In fact, Google's result prioritization algorithm, also known as its ranking algorithm, is attributed as the reason for its popularity. This ranking system merits further exploration, because it influences what we are likely to encounter on the Web.

RANKING SEARCH RESULTS

There are several (200) factors that influence the sequence of results when one conducts a web search using Google (Google, 2013). One important factor determines the significance of a web page, independent of its relevance to the search terms entered. This is called the *pageRank* (Strickland, 2008). Another factor assesses how well suited a page is to the search terms entered. We can call the two factors used for sequencing the search results *importance* (pageRank) and *suitability* and elaborate on each below.

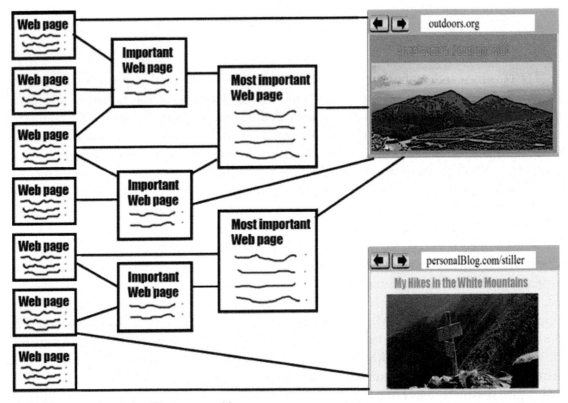

FIGURE 3.4 Illustrating a simplified page ranking

Importance of a Web Page

Figure 3.4 illustrates a simplified process for determining the importance of a web page. The sequence of steps necessary to carry out a calculation or some other determination is called an *algorithm*. The algorithm for determining the importance of a web page factors in the number of links to that page (Google, 2014). In Figure 3.4, all links are presumed to go from left to right. Looking at Figure 3.4, one can see that the web page *outdoors.org* has many more links going to it than the *personalBlog.com/stiller* web page. The algorithm also places a higher value on a link from a web page if the linking page also has links to it. For example, if a renowned travel website links to the outdoors.org page (presuming the travel site has a large number of links going to it), while the personal blog page has a family member linking a blog entry to it, the travel site's link would be considered a stronger endorsement. Figure 3.4 shows only three levels of importance, but in reality there are many more levels that factor into the algorithm. Since outdoors.org has many links from important web pages, and *personalBlog.com/stiller* has only two low-ranked web page links to it, the *outdoors.org* page would be considered more important and thus would be returned before the other page in search results. In the case of a search returning several hundred thousand results, this could mean the difference between residing on the first page versus page one-thousand. Entries on page one would likely be noticed, while those on page one-thousand would not likely be noticed.

Web Page Suitability

While page importance plays a large role in determining the ordering of search results, page suitability is also important. In the example, the search terms are *hiking* and *White Mountains*. These terms are not immediately obvious in the *outdoors.org* web page, whereas these terms appear in the heading of the *personalBlog.com/stiller* page. The suitability of a web page containing all search terms in its heading would make it more highly suitable than a web page where the search terms appear in text on the web page, but not in a heading. From this standpoint, the personal blog would be higher than the outdoors.org site, however since many references to the White Mountains and hiking are in the text of outdoors.org and it is a much more important website, the search would prioritize the outdoors.org page.

There is another important area where search terms may appear and thus influence the suitability of a web page. This area is called the metadata. Metadata, or data about data, is information embedded in the web page that does not appear on the page. Because the metadata is in the .html file, it can be analyzed to determine how suitable a web page is to matching the search criteria. An example of a metadata tag is shown below: <meta name="description" content="Learn about great hikes in the NH White Mountains from a local hiker."> Another important use of the description metadata is that the content field is used by search engines to describe the website in the search results.

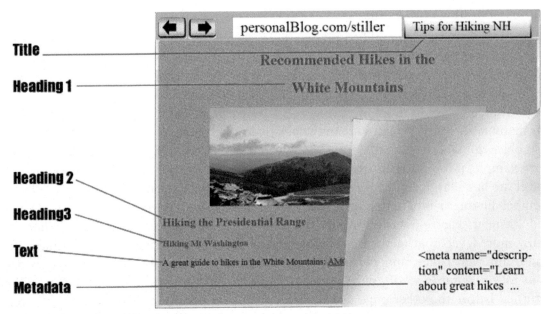

FIGURE 3.5 Illustrating different categories for search term placement

Figure 3.5 summarizes the different possibilities for identifying search terms on a web page, including three levels of headings (heading1, heading 2 and heading 3), the web page title, regular text, and metadata. If a search term is located in heading 1 (the largest heading) as opposed to regular text or a smaller heading (heading 2 or heading 3), this search term location would carry more weight when determining suitability. Many other factors are considered in the algorithm to order search results, and the considerations are adjusted to improve search quality on an ongoing basis. The preceding discussion is a highly simplified version of the algorithm, but is intended to provide a sense of how search engines prioritize results.

The results from search engines are very important from two perspectives. For someone seeking information, a search engine determines a likely pool of choices for one's knowledge quest. If the search results are skewed in some way, this has the potential of skewing one's understanding of the subject matter in question. From the standpoint of an individual or organization who wishes to be found on the Web, how a search functions is also very important. We will look at three phenomena that relate to web searches. One is link spamming. The second is promoting commercial interests, and the final is creating a context or profile for individuals searching and catering to the perceived interests of the person searching.

NEFARIOUS AND COMMERCIAL INFLUENCES ON WEB SEARCH

Because of the importance of where an entry appears in the list of search results, there are organizations and individuals who attempt to artificially influence this ordering. One way to influence this sequence is to pay the operators of a search engine for the privilege of appearing earlier. Another way to influence the ordering is to artificially manipulate the characteristics of a web page, so that the search ordering algorithm favors this page more than it should. No search engine operator would admit to allowing financial considerations to influence the sequence of search results, but all for profit search engines allow advertisers to appear on the results page. There is generally a visual distinction made between advertisements and search results, but this can be subtle. As someone looking for information, it is important to understand where the advertising ends and the search results begin.

One popular manipulation of search engine results plays on the central idea of Google's ranking system, which is the determination of the importance of a web page by analyzing links to this page, as previously described. Individuals who wish to manipulate the importance of a web page can generate fake links to that page. One way to generate fake links is to create a program that looks for blogs and adds comments that contain links to the web page to be elevated in ranking. This became such a problem that blogging systems had to incorporate a Completely Automated Public Turing Test to Tell Computers and Humans Apart (CAPTCHA) to protect blog comments from these programs. CAPTCHA asks people to interpret a distorted image of letters, something that would be computationally challenging for a program to do, but easy for a human.

Other ranking manipulations entail adding popular search terms to one or more of the more hidden areas like metadata or invisible text.

As someone who conducts searches, it is important to be aware that nefarious and commercial interests can change the results page. In the case of the commercial interests, one need only to be aware of the distinction between sponsored listing and search results. There is another important manipulation of search results that can have a profound influence on our democracy. This is something we should be aware of and possibly challenge. This search result manipulation is referred to as *filtering the web*.

FILTERING THE WEB

Filtering the web refers to the process of altering search results based on the perceived interests of the person conducting the search. In theory this is a handy service, if the perception is correct and depending on the criteria for the filtering. The primary issue is that we, as web searchers, have no control over this process and we are not shown the criteria for filtering.

In other words web filtering is not a transparent process. Another question worth asking is whether it is healthy for democracy to show people only results they like. An educated citizenry should be exposed a wide array of ideas, not simply those ideas that affirm what they already believe.

To illustrate how web filtering can be positive, when I entered *hiking* and *White Mountains* as search terms to conduct a search, my first page of results consisted only of links for the New Hampshire White Mountains, despite there being White Mountain ranges in other states. So, the search engine was providing me with results that are geographically close. The reason customization of results occurred is because when I access the search web page, the search engine analyzes my Internet Protocol (IP) address and locates my IP address geographically. When I connect to the Internet, my computer is assigned an IP address by the Internet Service Provider (ISP). It then uses this geographic context to select results close by. In this case I was interested in my neighboring mountain range, so the tailoring of results was desirable.

An example where the filtering of search results has a more troubling outcome was recounted by Eli Pariser during a TED talk (Pariser, 2011). Pariser asked a number of friends to enter *Egypt* into a Google web search and to send him an image of the first page of search results. Pariser recounted the results of two friends. One friend got results with links to sites discussing the current political crises in Egypt, while the other friend got travel information, but no information about a crisis in Egypt on his first page of results. Pariser affirmed that individuals are largely unaware of the tailoring of information during web

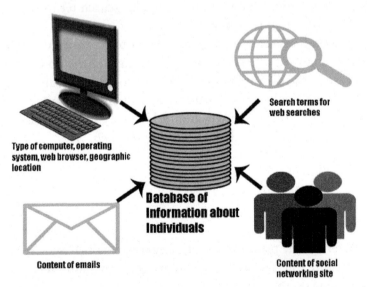

FIGURE 3.6 Information that can be used by search engines to customize results

searches and other information retrieval activities. The problem with filtering is that people are unaware that information it is being omitted and of the nature of what they are missing. This finding presumes that people rarely go beyond the first page or two of search results.

Figure 3.6 shows a number of information sources that search engines can use when tailoring results. Each search engine has its own algorithm for organizing search results, and not all search engines gather data on individuals conducting searches or extract information from emails. We will look at Google as the most popular search engine and the most notorious when it comes to data gathering about individual activity on the web. Figure 3.6 shows the following content areas for data gathering:

1. individual's computer, software, and IP address;
2. search terms that have been previously entered into the search engine;
3. the content of emails, if the search engine company also provides the email accounts; and
4. the content of social network data, if the search engine company runs the social network.

A search engine can determine from a basic Internet connection the model of the computer connecting, the operating system run by that computer, the web browser used to make the connection, and the IP address. The IP address can be further analyzed to determine a geographic location for the Internet connection, as previously mentioned. More information can be used. If the person has a history of using Google for searching and this person has installed other Google services, like the Google toolbar, Chrome, and Google Earth, Google has the ability to identify the user's machine uniquely using the media access control address (MAC address) and keep track of searches and other activities using Google's "free" services. The reason the word *free* is in quotation marks is to suggest that we do pay a price for free software, namely our privacy.

By incorporating details of someone's email and social media content, in conjunction with the previously mentioned information, like geographic location and previous search terms, one can paint a detailed picture of someone's interests. This might explain why one of Eli Pariser's friends got information about a political crisis in Egypt, while the other friend got travel information on their first page of search results.

Social Ramifications of Search

How individuals form their perception of reality is increasingly done from information found online. While not the only source of information on the Internet, search engines are an important means by which many people find information about the world. Consider for a moment the potential ramifications if people who have a conservative political bent see nothing but conservative perspectives when they research a topic and others who tend to be more liberal in their world view see nothing but liberal-minded perspectives. This method of filtering results would lend itself to people becoming increasingly more entrenched in

FIGURE 3.7 Can your web page be found by someone?

their mind-sets and less likely to find common ground with people who think differently. What compounds this situation is the fact that most people do not know that the information they get during web searches is customized for them.

At the very least we should be made aware of the information that is being used to characterize us and then used to alter our search results. It would be more desirable if the people conducting the search could view and alter the filtering criteria. If I wish to find a seafood restaurant, geographic filtering is desirable. If I am writing a paper on the Voting Rights Act, I wish to see all sides of the issue and not simply articles that affirm my own perspective. Current trends in filtering of web content suggest troubling practices. Perhaps in the coming years we can witness legislation that will make filtering more transparent, so we can at least elect to use search engines and other services that do not engage in secretive information filtering.

We have looked at the basic nuts and bolts of how the web works. To help cement the concepts the next section takes a concrete example that ties all the ideas together.

CAN *YOUR* INFORMATION BE FOUND ON THE WEB?

This section will provide a hypothetical but concrete example of creating web content and having that content found by someone who does not know the web developer. The web development scenario starts with someone who wishes to post information on a topic on a web page. For this example, we will assume the subject matter is something relatively unique so that the search engine does not return millions of competing websites. This presumes that your website is relatively new and therefore cannot have a volume of other web pages linking to it yet. Thus, the importance rating of a new website will always be low. In order to offset the poor importance rating, we must have few competitors when it comes to suitability.

Finding a unique topic on the web, given the sheer volume of information, is quite challenging. By selecting a very narrow and specific topic, like hiking Mount Morgan from the Cascade Trail, (an unmaintained trail) the chances of having little competition increases. The search terms would be "hiking Mount Morgan" and "Cascade Trail." A small note about conducting effective searches: enclosing the search terms in quotation marks directs the search engine to looks for that sequence of words. If the search terms are not enclosed in quotation marks, the search engine looks for the individual words in any sequence or context.

To ground our example of web development in reality, let us assume that the web developer is a student at Plymouth State University. The web developer would use a web page editing tool, like Amaya or Adobe Dreamweaver, to create a new web page and to create a title, heading, and/or metadata tag that would contain the topic of the web page. Of course the web developer would format the contents of the web page, select inviting colors, and include one or more images. The web developer would save the file containing the web page text and formatting instructions as an .html file (a file name having the extension .html) on his/her local machine before transferring it to the web server. Any images or other multimedia files must be saved with the .html file as well. The web developer would test the web page locally before transferring the files to the web server, as the page would then be potentially visible to the world. Although the definitive test of a web page is to access it through a web browser on a computer that does not have access to the web server files directly, one can open the web page on the local machine to correct content and formatting errors. On MS Windows machines, if you right-click on the .html file and select "open with" and then select the web browser of your choice, you can open a local file with a web browser.

Once the web page looks as desired on the local machine, the files can be transferred to the web server. In the case of the Plymouth State student/web developer, a campus machine provides access to a web-accessible directory on a special network-accessible drive. This particular web developer simply needs to copy all the files for the web page (.html and image files) to the web accessible folder. Other web developers would have to confer with their Internet Service Providers to determine how to transfer the files to the web server. The web page should be tested on the web server to make sure that the images and links still work as intended and that the web page layout is effective.

Once the content is available over the Internet, it can be accessed by anyone with an Internet connection. If someone is relying on a search engine to find the contents of your web page, the search engine must find your web page first, and put entries into the search database. Based on my own experience running a web server, I found that spiders visited my server relatively infrequently (about once a month), so depending on how many high-profile web pages reside on the web server containing your web page, it may take some time before information about your web page is available on one or more search engines.

Once your web page information is stored in the search engine database, and someone has a reason to search for your topic, then your page would be returned in the search results. To conclude our hypothetical web page example, someone in Kazakhstan reads an article about the lost trails of the White Mountains in NH and wishes to know more about the Cascade Trail ascending Mt. Morgan, because she has a cousin who lives in NH. She types "Mt. Morgan" and "Cascade Trail" into the search field of a search engine and gets a page back with only two results, and one of those results is from the student at Plymouth State. From the list of search results the person in Kazakhstan clicks on the link to the student's website, which contains the URL for the Mt Morgan Cascade Trail web page. This causes the Plymouth State web server to transmit the contents of this web page to the web browser requesting the information. The web browser uses the .html file and associated media files to format the content in the web browser window of the person in Kazakhstan.

Now that we have explored the process of placing information on the web and how this information can be found by people around the world, we will take our web page that we started in the previous chapter and turn it into a website by creating multiple linked web pages.

TRANSFORMING YOUR WEB PAGE INTO A WEBSITE

A website could consist of a single web page, but in general we think of websites as consisting of multiple interconnected and interrelated web pages. Although the topic of design does not appear as a primary topic until chapter six, we need to take into account some basic design principles before we have an abundance of content needing reworking. As we develop our websites by adding additional content, we want to observe one important design principle, that of *modularity*. We will explore the idea of modularity further in the design chapter, but we will discuss this notion briefly here.

Having a modular website suggests that as we add content, we will not simply create one very long web page, but rather create additional web pages that are linked together. Figure 3.8 illustrates a modular website. At the top of Figure 3.8 is the main web page,

FIGURE 3.8 Illustrating a modular design for a website

which introduces the subject matter of the website. In this case the topic for the website is "hiking in the White Mountains." The main page has links to other web pages that have more specific information on the topic. One link goes to a page that contains information about hiking mountains in the Presidential Range, while another link is to a page about hikes in the Squam Mountain Range and so on. Each page that is linked with the main page is called a *subpage,* and it contains information about a more specific topic under the umbrella topic specified by the main page.

In contrast to creating a modular website, a single long page requires extensive scrolling to reach all the content of interest. There are times when the long linear web page is an acceptable configuration, but until you are a more seasoned web developer, a modular design approach is a good beginning design strategy. A long linear web page can still contain links to subtopics within it, but for a visitor to the site, it can be confusing to identify when one topic begins and another ends.

HOW TO ADD PAGES TO YOUR WEBSITE

Because we are learning basic techniques of website creation, we will jump into the creation of a multiple-page website without the benefit of learning how to analyze and design websites. Website design will be discussed in later chapters, and content analysis is beyond the scope of this text. As you select content for each page, try to select content that supports a coherent subtopic within your website subject matter.

To create a subpage for your website:

1. Create a new web page.
2. Save the new page in the folder or subfolder of the main page.
3. Modify the main page to link to the new web page.

The steps for creating a new web page can be found in chapter two, so follow these instructions to create your subpage. Make sure that you save this web page in the same folder or subfolder of the main page. In order to transform the two independent web pages into a website, create a link from the main page to your subpage. Because we will want multiple subpages for our website we can set up the first link to be part of a list. In order to carry this out, you may do the following:

To create a link from your main web page to a subpage:

1. Open your main page in Amaya.
2. Place your cursor where you wish the ordered list to appear on your web page.
3. Select the menu items *Insert* → *List* → *Unordered List*.
4. Type a brief description of the content of the subpage. In the example, the text is "Great hikes in the Presidential range."
5. Select the text which will serve as the link to the subpage with your cursor and convert it to a link by selecting menu items *Links* → *Create or change link*.
6. A dialog box will pop up, as shown in Figure 3.11. Use the folder icon to navigate to the subpage.
7. Test your link by opening your main page in a web browser of your choice and clicking on your new link. Your new subpage should appear.
8. Create two to three additional subpages and repeat this process. Figure 3.12 shows a sample main page that links to 3 subpages.

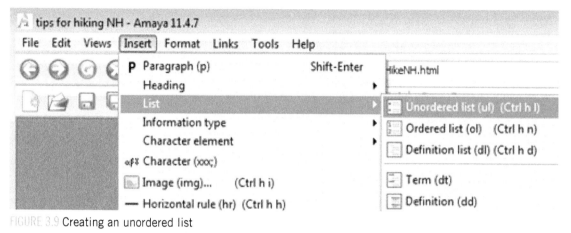

FIGURE 3.9 Creating an unordered list

Source: W3C / INRIA.

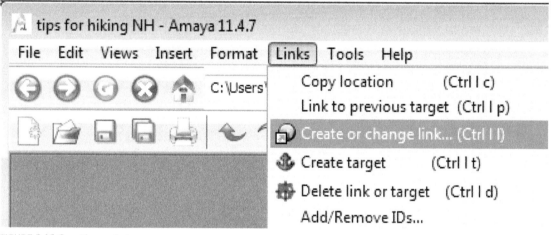

FIGURE 3.10 Creating a link

Source: W3C / INRIA.

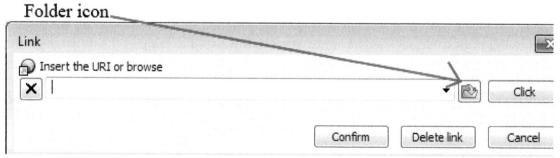

FIGURE 3.11 Selecting a linked web page: The text should now change color and be underlined, indicating that it is a link.

Source: W3C / INRIA.

FIGURE 3.12 Sample main page with list of links

SUMMARY

In this chapter, we explored the basic mechanics of how information is located on the Internet, including how web addresses are structured and are used to locate specific computers where information is stored. There is so much information available on the Internet that without a quality search engine, we would not be able to find high-quality information sources as easily. One important consideration when selecting a search engine is the algorithm that it uses to prioritize and order information on the results page. We should be mindful of possible skewing of information that we are receiving in the initial pages of our search results and take steps to broaden our exposure to a variety of perspectives. One periodic check we may wish to engage in is to check the results of our preferred search engine against another to see if there are any categories of information that we may be missing.

From the perspective of individuals using search engines we should consider what information is being gathered about us and how it might be used. Google is well-known for its data gathering. The searches we conduct can influence advertisements that appear on other websites we visit. Other possible uses of our search or other Internet activity are not clear and could have unforeseen consequences.

As developers of information on the Web, we can improve the likelihood of our websites being found by someone using a search engine when we consider how search engines prioritize results. If our websites are not well known, we need to create unique content in order to be found by most search engines. Using metadata and carefully crafting headings can help search engines prioritize our information.

REFERENCES

Google (2013). *How Search Works, from Algorithms to Answers*. Retrieved August 19, 2013 from http://www.google.com/intl/en_us/insidesearch/howsearchworks/thestory/

Netcraft (2013 August). *August 2013 Web Server Survey*. Retrieved August 15, 2013 from http://news.netcraft.com/archives/2013/08/09/august-2013-web-server-survey.html .

Pariser, E. (2011 May) *Beware online "filter bubbles."* [Video] May 2011. http://www.ted.com/talks/eli_pariser_beware_online_filter_bubbles.html, retrieved 8/20/2013.

Singer, N. (2013 August 17), "When You Can't Tell Web Suffixes Without a Scorecard", *New York Times*. Retrieved August 18, 2013 from http://www.nytimes.com/2013/08/18/technology/when-you-cant-tell-web-suffixes-without-a-scorecard.html?hp&_r=0

Strickland, J.(2008 January) *Why is the Google algorithm so important?*. January 11, 2008. HowStuffWorks.com. Retrieved April 28, 2014 from http://computer.howstuffworks.com/google-algorithm.htm.

CHAPTER FOUR

THE DARK SIDE OF THE INTERNET: VIRUSES, SPYWARE, IDENTITY THEFT, AND THE LOSS OF PRIVACY

POINTS TO CONSIDER

- What are the qualities of a good netizen?
- What are some rules of good netiquette?
- What is malware?
- Give 5 examples of malware and explain each.
- How can you protect yourself from the various types of malware?
- What dangers can email embody?
- What is phishing?

- What safe email practices should one observe?
- How do spammers get email addresses?
- How are cookies useful?
- How could cookies be harmful?
- Could cookies contain viruses?
- How should cookies most effectively be handled?

WHY SHOULD WE CONSIDER THE DANGERS OF THE INTERNET?

As web developers we are engaged in two basic activities that can make us vulnerable to malicious elements of the Internet. We are putting content on the web and taking shared content from the web. As a result, we must be mindful about the potential risks that we take as we build our websites. In addition to downloading shared images from the web, we may choose to install software, such as web development tools, programming languages, image and sound editing tools, and video development software. The most risky activity that we can engage in is the installation of software, so we need to know how to do this safely.

This chapter discusses the dangerous aspects of the Internet that we should be aware of and how we can take steps to minimize these risks. The chapter will begin by looking at considerations concerning the content we place on the Internet and then explore risks we encounter as we download resources.

ETHICAL WEB DEVELOPMENT AND PRIVACY PROTECTION

As we develop content for the web, there are considerations beyond the violation of copyright that we need to be aware of. As web developers we should strive to be good *netizens*, that is, good citizens on the Internet. There are certain principles of good *netiquette* (network etiquette) that we should keep in mind as we plan our websites. Because the focus of this text is web development and not other forms of Internet-based communication like emails, chats, and other online forums, a subset of netiquette rules will be discussed. The rules can be summarized as follows:

1. Think about your audience.
2. Represent yourself in a positive manner, and think about your future self.
3. Think about your own privacy, and watch out for spam bots.
4. Do not violate the privacy of others.
5. Do not take the intellectual property of others.
6. Divulge any conflicts of interest you have.
7. Do not perpetuate stereotypes.
8. Do not misrepresent reality.

The first rule places the audience in the forefront of our website development. As we develop website content, we should keep in mind that people from around the world are possibly visiting our website, not just a handful of friends and family members. Therefore, we should write clearly and professionally and use correct spelling and grammar. We should also explain images or other multimedia content, rather than assume a common point of reference. Finally, we should keep individuals in mind who have slower Internet connection speeds and should include the smallest file sizes with adequate quality for any multimedia files. More detail will be provided in subsequent chapters regarding how to reduce the file size of various multimedia content.

Rule number two suggests that the content of a website reflects on the developer of that site. This provides additional motivation to use clear and professional language in addition to creating well-crafted and thoughtful multimedia content. The website should suggest that the developer is a mature and intelligent person. One should not include self-images that are unflattering, or would cause a prospective employer to have second thoughts about hiring you. Although the content of a website can be changed at any time, we do not have control over organizations that archive web contents. For example, web.archive.org archives websites and makes these archived sites available over the Internet. We do not know which organizations may also engage in archiving in the future, possibly without our knowledge. This means that content that we post may haunt us in the future, so we should take care to represent ourselves positively at all times.

In addition to the possibility of web content persisting beyond our control, it is being processed by computer programs to find marketable data such as email addresses and other personal information. Spam-bots scour the Web looking for email addresses, which are then used to generate spam. Spam is defined as unrequested email solicitations that are sent in bulk. If it can be avoided, emails and other personal information should not be included in websites. It may be necessary, however, to provide visitors to your website a means to contact you. In this case, email addresses can be embedded in images so that they are less likely to be recognized by computer programs and yet are readily understood by humans.

It is important to guard the privacy of individuals by not including their names or images of them on your website without their permission. People who are public officials or celebrities may be mentioned and depicted, because their public status compromises their expectation to privacy. This allows for critique, adulation, or other reference of these individuals.

Guideline number five reminds us to respect the intellectual property of others. This concept was emphasized in chapter one and so will not be elaborated upon here.

Guideline number six suggests that website authors should divulge any conflicts of interest. For example, if you author a website or blog that rates consumer electronics and you accept advertising revenue from such a manufacturer, this should be disclosed to the readers. Also, if you have a political leaning and this is pertinent to your website, this should also be made clear so that readers can factor the information into the substance of the site.

In the spirit of reflecting positively upon yourself, the seventh guideline discourages the perpetuation of stereotypes. These can be gender-based, race-based, based on ethnicity, based on being able-bodied, or based on gender identification or expression. Thus, women and racial minorities should not be portrayed as inferior in any manner, and one should not express derogatory opinions of groups of individuals.

The final guideline requires us to be conscientious about people's perception of reality. Unless the website is humorous or a spoof site, the content presented should be accurate to the best of the author's knowledge. If content is speculative, it should be represented as such. Also, edited images on the site that may be perceived as representing reality should be labeled as having been altered.

Now that guidelines for content have been enumerated, we will explore the dangers one may encounter as one retrieves resources from the Internet. We will start with the most perilous activity, downloading software.

HOW TO INSTALL SOFTWARE SAFELY

When it pertains to protecting the integrity of one's computer, the most dangerous activity one can engage in is downloading and installing software. Installing software is a critical activity when it comes to web development. Software like web page editors, image editors, sound editors, animation software, and computer programming languages can facilitate the creation of engaging websites. However, while one may believe that legitimate software is being installed, one may be installing malware. *Malware* is an umbrella term that refers to any software that is harmful. Examples of malware are viruses, spyware, key loggers, and Trojan horses.

The key to installing software safely is to get software from a reputable source. There is useful software that is freely available, but individuals who intend to distribute malware often masquerade as organizations distributing legitimate software. One can search the web for information about the site distributing the software and closely scrutinize the URL of the site to ensure that you are at the correct site. Also, safeweb.norton.com rates websites for their safety, so one can check the website distributing the software at this or similar sites.

There are well-known websites that distribute software. For example, you can download free open source software at SourceForge.com. Software like GIMP can be downloaded at SourceForge.com and a series of other reputable sites, but it is possible that malicious websites could disseminate a modified version that contains a virus. Before you select a source for your software, check this site.

The reason installing software is so dangerous is that when one installs software, certain protections are overridden in this process. Once the executable file is on the computer and is run, it can replicate itself, delete files, install other malicious software, or modify existing applications to malfunction. This software can take a number of forms, so a brief synopsis of possible types of malware is provided below.

Viruses

The name for software viruses was inspired by their similarity with biological viruses. The similarities that both types of viruses share are as follows:

1. harm the host (human or computer);
2. replicate themselves;
3. are passed from host to host;
4. can be dormant and then attack at a later time

Viruses can be embedded in software that initially operates as expected. This initial correct functioning may allow the virus to be spread to other computers as the software is shared between individuals. When the software is run, the virus may modify other software, operating system files, or data files to contain the virus or to become unusable. These changes can make the computer inoperable or cause data loss. Not all viruses disrupt operations in this manner, however. They may instead carry a message of some sort, communicate private information to the virus authors, or generate spam email.

Anti-virus software exists to eradicate viruses or prevent their destructive behavior. However, new viruses emerge constantly and virus protection software can only identify known viruses. Consequently, even with up-to-date virus detection software, one could still fall prey to virus infection.

Spyware

Spyware refers to a category of malicious software that transmits personal information to an unintended party without the knowledge of the victim. This information can take the form of financial information, passwords or Internet browsing habits. Spyware can also redirect browser traffic to unwanted sites. For example, if one does a search for a topic, spyware can either populate the search results with substitute results, like pornography sites or sites selling counterfeit pharmaceuticals. Alternatively, the search results can appear to be legitimate, but when one clicks on a link, the links take one to an unintended site. Spyware is often unwittingly installed with seemingly legitimate software.

Keystroke Loggers

Keystroke loggers are a form of spyware that transmits each key stroke that is pressed on the keyboard of an infected computer. This form of virus can lead to monetary or identity theft, because if the unwitting victim of the logger engages in financial transactions or uses passwords using the infected computer, this information will be transmitted to the distributers of the malicious software. Because keystroke loggers capture each keystroke, the encryption provided by financial services or other sites cannot prohibit the transmission of this information. As a result credit card information can be gathered in addition to other personal information that can lead to identity theft.

Computer Worms

Computer worms are a form of malware similar to computer viruses in that they can replicate themselves and spread from computer to computer. The primary distinguishing features are that they do not attach themselves to or modify other data or software files. Their primary harm is the consumption of computer resources, such as network bandwidth and computer memory. They can cause financial loss by consuming enough resources that they prohibit legitimate work from being performed on the computers.

Trojan Horses

A Trojan horse is a form of malware that does not replicate itself, but is installed with seemingly legitimate software, a ploy similar to the legend of the Trojan horse. In the legend Greek soldiers were smuggled into the city of Troy by hiding in a giant wooden horse statue. Similarly, malicious software is installed under the guise of legitimate software. In addition to destroying various computing resources, a Trojan horse program can also install a program, called a backdoor, that allows people access to the computer without the owner's consent. The backdoor program can be used to orchestrate other attacks, disseminate spam email, or conduct other malicious activity.

In addition to the possibility of unintentionally installing malicious software, other dangers exist on the Internet. We will investigate spam and phishing next.

HOW TO USE EMAIL SAFELY

Email can be a means by which all sorts of individuals contact you. Many of these contacts are desired, but others range from an annoying cluttering of your email inbox to attempts at stealing your identity. There are a number of means by which one can reduce the number of annoying or malicious emails one receives by using a filter. Filters are not fool proof and if one's friend's or family member's email account has been compromised, a malicious email could come from a trusted person.

Spam and Phishing

People who distribute spam may be engaging in mass marketing or trying to steal your identity. Spammers can get email addresses in a number of ways. They can purchase lists from other organizations, randomly generate addresses, or scour the web for email addresses posted on web pages (recall the mention of spam in the section on ethical web development). Random email generation consists of computer-generated email names affixed to known email domains, like gmail.com or yahoo.com. If a randomly generated email address does not belong to an individual, an email error message will be sent. If no error is generated, the spammer can add this address to a list of legitimate addresses.

Spamming with malicious intent is known as *phishing*. Phishing attempts use social-engineering techniques to get individuals to divulge private information. Social engineering techniques exploit information about how organizations or individuals behave to trick them into divulging information such as credit card numbers, social security numbers, or other sensitive information that could be used to establish bank accounts, credit cards, or file for tax returns.

Phishing can also be predicated on shear volume. Rather than relying on knowledge of specific individuals, such a large number of emails is sent that a small percentage of responses is of value. For example, emails offering to resolve insufficient email storage capacity, expiring credit cards, or other financial account glitches are commonplace. The emails are formulated to be very specific. For example, the email may contain the logo and name of a specific bank and indicate that, due to excessive attempts to login, a change of password and account number is advised. The email either links you to a site where your current account information can be submitted so that a new account can be generated or the email itself may allow this information to be entered. Of course, one should never divulge sensitive information as a result of an email solicitation.

Phishing emails can be very convincing, if one happens to have accounts with the organization that the scammers are masquerading as. Certain organizations offer phishing quizzes so that people can test their ability to distinguish between legitimate emails and phishing attempts. One such organization is http://www.sonicwall.com/furl/phishing/. One cannot rely on the wording or graphics of the email as a clue to its legitimacy. The best way to authenticate an email is to scrutinize the URL of any embedded links to determine if it contains the legitimate domain. Even better, one should never respond directly to such an email solicitation. If there is a problem with your bank account, navigate to the bank's website without using links from an email. That is the safest way to operate.

A final category of email-based scam is one in which a friend's or family member's email account information has been compromised. You could receive a solicitation for money from the legitimate account of someone you know. The current scam involves the person you know losing a wallet while on vacation and needing your assistance. The only trouble is that a scammer is behind the scenes ready to steal your money. Should you receive any solicitation for money, you should attempt to contact that person via a familiar telephone number, not one provided by the email.

Phishing attempts have become so pervasive that many financial institutions no longer embed links in emails to customers. For example, in order to prompt customers to pay their monthly credit card bill, several banks issue an email reminder with enough identifying information to assure the recipient that the source of the email is legitimate. These email reminders do not include links to the banking site, so customers navigate to the banking site independently from the email. In order to be safe, the practice of never navigating to financial sites via email links is advisable.

Links and Attachments in Spam and Malicious Emails

Here is more incentive to avoid clicking on links embedded in emails unless you know the source and the contents are clearly from this person. Always remember that email accounts can be hacked. Another form of malicious email exists aside from phishing attempts. These malicious emails contain links to executable files that could cause your web browser to execute undesired instructions and thereby give hackers control over your computer. Another similar type of malicious link is an attempt to trick you into believing that your computer is already infected, using alarming graphics, and then offering you free anti-virus software, which is really a virus. Finally, attachments should be opened with caution, because they may contain malicious executable files or other file types that attempt to take control of the computer.

One should never open an attachment with an .exe file extension, but even a .pdf attachment could contain instructions that could cause the pdf reader to malfunction and thereby leave your computer vulnerable to takeover by hackers. Similarly, links could connect to scripts with .php extensions that could cause the browser to malfunction or modify browser settings in undesirable ways, like setting your home page to an undesired commercial site.

In addition to safety concerns pertaining to downloading information from the Internet and emailing, individuals should be aware of information that is being recorded about their web browsing habits.

HOW TO SURF THE WEB SAFELY

When we use a web browser to visit websites, these websites are writing records of our activity on our computers. These bits of information are known as *cookies*. Cookies are often necessary to carry out certain web-based transactions, like purchasing items from a website. For example, cookies can keep track of a list of items when one is making purchases at a retail site. So, in this regard they are a necessity to make conducting business on the web possible. On the other hand, cookies can also be used to track which websites we have visited for the purpose of selecting advertisements to post. The second form of cookie could compromise our privacy. Additionally, cookies can be used maliciously, so they deserve further discussion here.

Cookies

Cookies are text files that can be written to our computers through web browsers and are therefore also known as *HTTP cookies*. Because web browsers write the cookies, the harm that can be perpetrated through this process is limited, since web browsers are designed to have limited access to files. Each web browser determines where cookies are written. Each browser also limit cookie files to being text-based, as opposed to executable. The fact that cookies are text in format, rather than executable, means that they cannot execute a malicious function like deleting or corrupting files. Cookies can, however, still be used in a malicious manner.

In order to better understand how cookies are used, the specific types of cookies will be discussed. There are two basic categories of cookies, *session cookies* and *persistent/tracking cookies*. Session cookies keep track of information that result from a person's activities on a particular web page, so that this information isn't lost when a subsequent page is visited. To understand this better think of a shopping cart function at a particular commercial site. As we gather items to buy at a site, this information can be recorded in a session cookie. Session cookies, as the name implies, persist for the duration of the transaction. Once the web-based service is completed, any session cookies are deleted. Because of their short duration, session cookies are not the primary concern for malicious activity.

Persistent Cookies

Persistent cookies, including *third-party cookies,* are of primary concern for possible malicious activity. Third-party cookies are those set by a site other than the one that you are currently viewing. Third-party cookies often come from advertisers, so persistent cookies can result in targeted advertisements. For example, in the experience of this author, after looking up the location of a golf course using a popular search engine, I now receive advertisements for golf merchandise whenever I go to a particular weather website.

There are legitimate reasons for creating persistent cookies. Some cookies could be useful for the person visiting the website. For example, certain commercial sites can customize the website to cater to your previous purchases or interests. For example, if one had ordered a mystery novel from a book retailer, one might expect to find recommendations for other mystery books upon a later visit to that website. Sites that offer to "remember" login information also use cookies, but it should be noted that the actual user name and password are not stored in clear text, but instead are encoded so that third-parties cannot steal this information.

Taking Action Against Malicious Cookies

Because cookies are text-only and written through the web browser, damage done by them is limited. The primary issue concerning cookies is that they store private information that other websites could access. Websites that use cookies appropriately do not store information that could be used to compromise your privacy or steal your identity.

Web browsers allow the specification of privacy settings, including how cookies should be handled. It is possible to block all cookies by certain web browsers, but this would limit some desired web services like shopping carts and website customization. Most web browsers allow blocking third-party cookies while permitting other cookies. If your preferred web browser allows the blocking of third-party cookies, this is advisable. It is also a good idea to periodically delete cookies. The possible undesired side-effect of deleting cookies is that certain websites lose their customization.

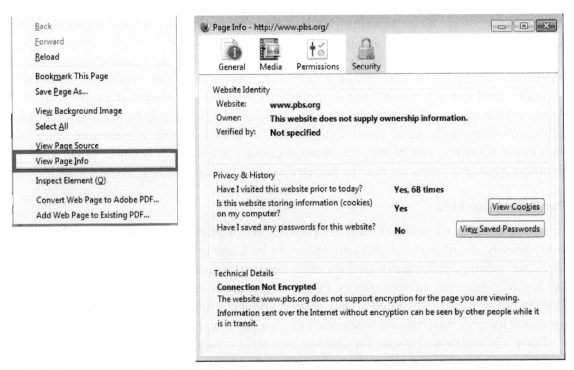

FIGURE 4.1 How to view cookies in Mozilla Firefox

Source: Mozilla Corporation.

How one checks and/or deletes cookies varies by web browser and possibly web browser version. For instructions on the up-to-date procedure for inspecting/deleting cookies, one can search the web for these instructions. In order to have a sense of how this can be done, using Mozilla Firefox, a brief scenario is provided here. In Firefox one right-clicks on a particular web page and a menu that looks like the one shown on the left-hand side of Figure 4.1 appears. Selecting the menu option, *View Page Info* causes a dialog to appear. When one selects the *Security* tab, as shown in the window in the right-hand side of Figure 4.1, a button that allows one to view cookies is shown. When one clicks on this button, the cookies for that website are listed. Specific cookies may be viewed by clicking on them. Cookies may also be deleted as a group. Changing the contents of the search field at the top of the *Cookies* window allows cookies from other sites to be viewed. To see all cookie folders, delete all contents from the search field and then press the enter key.

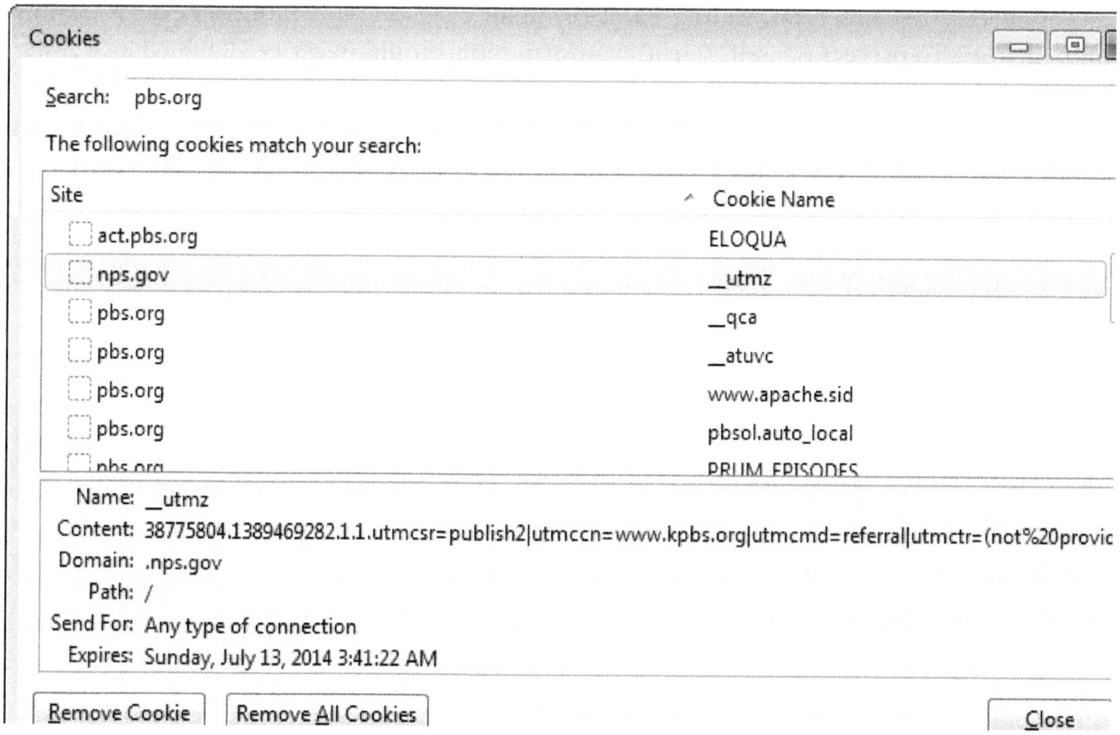

FIGURE 4.2 Managing cookies in Mozilla Firefox

Source: Mozilla Corporation.

SUMMARY

As web developers, we should be careful about the content we place on our websites as well as the content we access over the Internet. When developing content for our websites, we should be mindful about our and others' privacy. We should strive to reflect positively on ourselves and provide useful and accurate information to others. We should also take care to avoid perpetuating stereotypes with our web content.

The most dangerous activity one may engage in is the downloading of software. At the same time, installing freely available software over the Internet, like Amaya and GIMP, is highly desirable. Such programs can make web development much easier. When selecting software to download, it is important to select a site that is reputable to void installing malware. A number of different types of malware exist and can result in everything from a minor annoyance to identity theft or one's computer functioning as a server to send out malicious emails.

Other activities besides downloading and installing software can have equally harmful effects. Email can take the form of spam or phishing attempts. The goal of phishing is to take monetary resources by stealing bank or credit card account numbers or by stealing one's identity. To protect oneself, sensitive information should never be divulged as a result of an email solicitation.

A final consideration covered in this chapter is the bits of information our web browsers record about our web browsing habits, known as cookies. Because they are text-based files, they are not executable and can never contain a virus or other malware. While cookies can be useful, they can also be an invasion of our privacy, and it is advisable to be aware of the cookies on your computer.

CHAPTER FIVE

HOW COMPUTERS REPRESENT IMAGES: CREATING EFFECTIVE IMAGES ON THE WEB

POINTS TO CONSIDER

- What is the difference between a digital and an analog representation of information, e.g. time?
- Why do digital computers use the binary system?
- How does the binary system work?
- How is the binary system similar to the decimal system?
- What is a bit/byte?
- How are images represented digitally?
- What is RGB?
- Why do different image file formats exist?
- What are the strengths and weaknesses of JPEG, GIF and PNG respectively?
- What is interlacing?
- What is dithering and why would one use this approach to color expression?
- What is color depth?

- Are images embedded in HTML files?
- Does resizing an image on a web page using a web page editor change the size of the image file?
- Which schools of ethical thought apply to image editing/selection?
- Which principles from National Press Photographers Association code of ethics apply to image editing/selection?
- How did *The Daily News* violate professional ethics in the story of the Boston Marathon bombing?
- What other examples of violations of professional ethics by the mass-media as a result of photo editing are you aware of?
- What is an image map? How can one be effectively used on a website?

INTRODUCTION

One may wonder how a device like a computer, which was originally designed to make numerous calculations very quickly, is able to represent things like images, sounds, animations, and videos. The manner in which a computer represents images is similar to how it represents numbers. A computer represents everything as numbers because it is a digital device as opposed to an analog device. Figure 5.1 illustrates the distinction between a digital clock and an analog clock. The digital clock expresses time as discrete numbers, like 8:09. The analog clock, by contrast, has a continuous representation of time as the clock hands sweep from number to number. An analog clock can express a fractional minute as the minute hands moves between numbers. It is up to us to interpret the position of the hands as a partial minute. The digital clock represents one minute as a distinct number. If we look at a digital clock, we do not know if the next minute will appear immediately or in another 59 seconds. Of course, one could argue that a digital clock could have a representation for seconds, but we are comparing equivalent analog and digital clocks. Both have an hour and minute representation. In digital computers, just as there is a coding system for representing different numbers, there is a coding system for representing different colors. These colors are the building blocks of images, videos, and animations.

The Binary System

Because computers are electronic devices, they are well suited for representing two states, high voltage and low voltage. As a result, computers can easily represent information with two values like true/false, yes/no, or one/zero. The high voltage state of a transistor represents the value one, while the low voltage state represents zero. The number system that consists of these two numbers is the binary system. The binary system works like the decimal system. The binary system is called the base-2 system, while the decimal system is called the base-10 system.

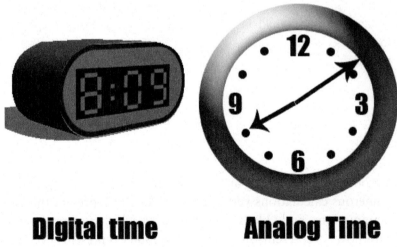

Digital time   **Analog Time**

FIGURE 5.1 Showing the distinction between digital and analog time

The decimal system consists of ten numbers, 0 through 9. In a decimal number each digit from right to left represents a progressively higher power of ten. For example, in the decimal value 1264, the value 4 is multiplied by 10^0, which has the value 1; the value 6 is multiplied by 10^1, which has the value 10; the value 2 is multiplied by 10^2, which has the value 100, and the value 1 is multiplied by 10^3, which has the value 1000. The respective products are then added as follows: 4 + 60 + 200 +1000, producing 1264.

The binary system works in a similar manner to the decimal system. The only differences are that there are only two values, namely zero and one, to work with and that each binary digit is multiplied by a power of two, rather than ten. So, a binary number might look like 10110101. Reading the digits from right to left, each binary digit is multiplied by a higher power of two, starting with 2^0, which has the value 1. Since the binary digits with the value zero will produce the result zero no matter what power of two they are multiplied by, we can simply add the powers of two that are associated with the ones in the binary number. The sample binary number,10110101 is evaluated as $2^0+2^2+2^4+2^5+2^7$. This calculation translates to 1+4+16+32+128, or 181. Figure 5.2 illustrates the connection between the voltage level of transistors and the numeric value they represent. Each transistor with high voltage represents the value 1 while those with low voltage represent the value 0. The transistors work together to determine a numeric value. The transistors represent a progressively higher power of two, just as with binary numbers. So, the figure illustrates how the binary number could be represented using electronic components.

Now that we have explored basic information representation in computers, we can now look at how images are represented.

REPRESENTING IMAGES

Expressing numeric values using computer circuits can be readily done, but how does one represent aqua marine, burnt orange, or violet magenta? First, computers require connected devices that can display or print the colors in question for the representation of colors to be meaningful. A computer monitor can serve as our device for expressing color. A monitor is composed of a rectangular configuration of pixels. A pixel is the smallest area that can be assigned a color. The color of a pixel is determined by the values assigned to its red, green, and blue elements. Figure 5.3 shows a hypothetical monitor displaying an image. One can zoom in on an image until the pixels comprising that image are shown as individual blocks of color, as in the magnified area in Figure 5.3. The figure also provides the values for the amount of red, green, and blue light for one selected pixel in the image.

As with computer representations of numbers, color representations are rooted in the binary nature of computers. Another important set of terms when it comes to computer

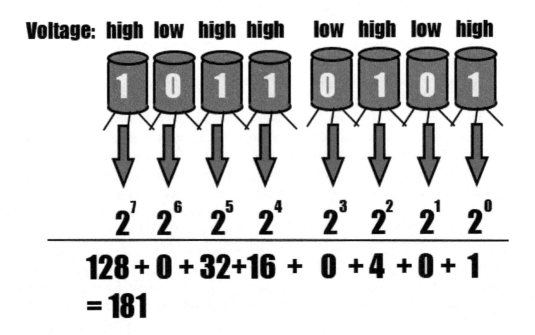

FIGURE 5.2 Illustrating the connection between digital circuitry and representing numbers

FIGURE 5.3 Zooming in on an image to reveal individual pixels

representation of information is *bit* and *byte*. A bit is a single 0/1 value. A bit is the value that a single transistor can store, as shown in Figure 5.2. A byte is a collection of bits that together represent a piece of information, as the eight bits in Figure 5.3 represent the decimal value 181. A common size for a byte is eight bits. The concept of a bit is important when discussing color representations, because certain color formats specify a *color depth*, which is the number of bits used to express the values of red, green, and blue (RGB) when activating a pixel.

On a computer, images are stored in files and consist of a rectangular configuration of color specifications that can be assigned to the pixels of a computer monitor. There are a variety of image file formats that can be used. Some common file formats are BMP, JPEG, PNG, GIF, and WebP.

Image-File Formats

Our discussion of image-file formats will focus on a category of image formats known as *raster*. A raster image representation involves a pixel oriented specification of color. The other category of image formats is known as *vector*. Vector images are represented mathematically, as a set of geographic shapes, locations, dimensions, and colors. As a result, vector images are very efficient, but not suitable for photorealistic images. Vector images require special software to produce and display them. Because animation software often uses vector graphics, this topic will be deferred until the animation chapter.

The main reason that understanding image file formats is important is so we can make informed decisions about the images we use in our websites. Our goal is to have high-quality images, and to use network capacity wisely. In other words, we should not use images on our websites that are unnecessarily large, because this will cause our web pages to download slowly, especially for those who have slower Internet connections. So, efficient image representation is central to our discussion.

BMP

The bitmap (BMP) image format is the simplest type of raster image, but it is also inefficient. Although BMP files can be found on the web, they are not a good choice for websites because these files are unnecessarily large. A BMP file has an entry for every pixel in the image, and so is a simple format to understand. The other raster image file formats discussed here use some form of compression algorithm to summarize a group of pixels and are therefore more efficient and better suited for use on websites.

Figure 5.4 illustrates a partial representation of a BMP file, where the values for five pixels are shown. Each pixel is expressed as three numeric values in sequence surrounded by brackets to separate the values of one pixel from another. The first number represents how much red is used to create the color. The second number determines the quantity of green, and the final value specifies how much blue there is in the color. Each RGB value is between *0* and *255*. This is the value range, because eight bits are used to represent each color element. Because RGB has three colors comprising each pixel, a total of *24* bits are required to specify one pixel. So this particular representation has a color depth of 24.

Red, Green, Blue shown as (#,#,#)

[103,91,95] [133,125,148] [184,180,215] [184,180,215] [184,180,21!

FIGURE 5.4 Showing the pixel representation of five pixels in sequence

TABLE 5.1 Characteristics of some common file formats

IMAGE FORMAT	COMPRESSION	SUPPORTS TRANSPARENCY	SUPPORTS ANIMATION	LOSES ACCURACY	INTERLACED
BMP	None	No	No	No	No
GIF	Best with line drawings	Yes	Yes	No	Yes
JPEG	Best with photorealistic	No	No	Yes	Yes
PNG	Best with line drawings	Yes	Yes	No	Yes

In Figure 5.4, the first two pixels are of different colors, while the last three pixels are the same color, repeated three times. In BMP files, this repeated color would be written in the file, whether there were three repetitions or one million. Other raster file formats would employ an algorithm to create a more concise representation for the repeated values, known as a *compression algorithm*. The strategy behind the compression algorithm used by

JPEG, PNG and GIF respectively, determines what kind of images they can most efficiently represent, so it merits a cursory look at these algorithms.

JPEG, PNG, and GIF

JPEG stands for Joint Photographic Experts Group; PNG stands for Portable Network Graphics, and GIF stands for Graphics Interchange Format. Unlike the BMP format, these formats do not encode color of each individual pixel, but attempt to represent repeated or similar colors more concisely to create smaller file sizes. The way a particular file format compresses a file determines what kind of images a format is best suited to represent.

GIF is a file format that compresses files by creating a concise representation of areas of repeated color. This type of compression is most effective with line drawings, because line drawings generally contain large swaths of the same color. As a result, the GIF format is not very effective for compressing photorealistic images, because these images contain many subtle variations of a color rather than repeated areas of the same color. GIF file compression does not lose any information. In other words, an exact pixel by pixel recreation of an image is possible after image compression.

The GIF format also supports animation, by allowing a series of images to be recorded and played one after the other to simulate motion. GIF also supports transparency. Although all raster image files are defined as a rectangular area, GIF formatted images can appear to have a non-rectangular shape because of areas of transparency.

The PNG image format was created because the GIF format was originally patented, though the patent has now expired. PNG shares the above characteristics of GIF, and can have greater color depth than GIF. GIF format images are limited to a color depth of eight, or 256 colors. PNG allows a variable color depth of up to twenty-four. Colors not included in the 256 colors in GIF or PNG can be simulated by interleaving colors that could be mixed to create that color. Figure 5.5 illustrates this color interleaving, known as *dithering*, by showing red and yellow blocks of color in smaller and smaller configurations until orange seems to emerge.

In contrast to GIF and PNG, which are most effective at compressing images with large areas of the same color, the JPEG format is best suited to representing photorealistic images where there are many different shades of colors in close proximity. The JPEG algorithm looks for information that can be summarized without a visually perceptible loss of quality. The algorithm utilizes information from psycho-visual research to reduce the file size and still retain the perceived quality of the image. JPEG images do not support transparency, so they will always take a rectangular visual form. They also do not support animation.

One final property shared by JPEG, GIF, and PNG is *interlacing*. An interlaced image is downloaded over the web in multiple passes. This results in an image that initially appears to be blurry on a web page, but becomes progressively clearer as the web page completes downloading. This allows a viewer to have a sense of the content of an image almost immediately, while requiring a small amount of additional time to deliver a crisp image.

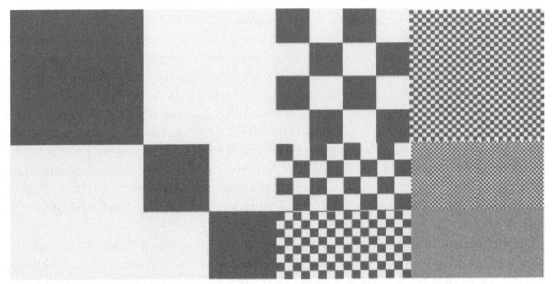

FIGURE 5.5 The red and yellow squares are smaller and smaller until orange appears

Table 5.2 illustrates the file sizes of the key file formats discussed so far as applied to a photorealistic image and a line drawing of equal dimension. While inspecting the various file sizes, be sure to note the distinction between *MB* and *KB*. MB stands for million bytes, while KB stands for thousand bytes. The second column of the table illustrates the sizes for a photorealistic image. As one would expect, the JPEG file is the smallest, since its compression algorithm is best suited to this type of image. The JPEG is about half the size of the next smallest file. The BMP format is by far the largest for both images, since no compression occurs in the photorealistic image. BMP does support some compression in line drawings by reducing the color depth.

The third column in Table 5.2 shows the files sizes for a sample line drawing. As would be expected in this case, PNG and GIF are much smaller than the JPEG. Another noteworthy point is that despite the line drawing being of the same dimensions as the photorealistic image, the files sizes are considerably smaller, independent of image format.

TABLE 5.2 Comparing file sizes among different image formats

IMAGE TYPE	PHOTOREALISTIC	LINE DRAWING
Sample thumbnail		
Original size	2592 ↔ 1944 pixels	2592 ↔ 1944 pixels
BMP	14.4 MB	4.8 MB
GIF	2.66 MB	69.1 KB
JPEG	1.16 MB	225 KB
PNG-8	2.29 MB	28.7 KB
PNG-24	6.45 MB	32.9 KB

One important consideration when adding images to a web page is to ensure that the image file format is efficient for the type of image being used. A more important consideration is image size. This topic will be briefly addressed next.

IMPORTANCE OF IMAGE SIZE

Web page editing tools, like Amaya and Adobe Dreamweaver, can resize images that are embedded in web pages. Recall, however, that the image is only referenced by a web page, so the process of adding and resizing an image specifies a reference to the image along with its desired dimensions. The original image file is still downloaded without altered dimensions, independent of the displayed size. So, a JPEG image used directly from a digital camera could have dimensions exceeding the size of a typical computer monitor. If such an image is embedded in a web page using the resizing of the web page editor (this does not shrink the image itself), an excessively large image is being downloaded, and could cause an unnecessarily long download time.

In order to create a more efficient web page, it is important to resize the image to approximately the desired display size before adding it to a web page. Fine tuning of the dimensions of an image in the web page editor is expected. Table 5.3 indicates the file size of a JPEG image of varying dimensions to illustrate the effect of image size on file size. A 500 by 350 pixel image is shown with a 250 by 188 pixel image embedded to illustrate the approximate size of these images. If you wish to show large, high resolution images on a website, you may wish to show a table of thumbnail images and allow visitors to your website to select which of the large images to view, given the potentially long download times.

TABLE 5.3 Comparing image dimensions and file size

Sample 500 ↔ 350 and 250 ↔ 188 pixel image

Original dimensions	3264 ↔ 2448	1000 ↔ 750	500 ↔ 350	250 ↔ 175
File size	5.65 MB	868 KB	234KB	63.9 KB

The ability to resize an image is an important feature of image editing software, but there are many others capabilities of this class of software worth exploring here. Before addressing other aspects of image editing software, we will explore the ethics of image creation and manipulation.

THE ETHICS OF IMAGE SELECTION AND MANIPULATION

This section addresses two questions. First, are there ethical concerns about posting images to a website? Second, can some alterations to an image be considered unethical? Concerns of copyright have already been addressed in chapter one, so the ethical concerns to be discussed here do not pertain to questions of intellectual property ownership. An in-depth treatment of ethics is beyond the scope of this text, but a brief introduction to applicable schools of thought will be provided.

Basic Ethical Perspectives

The two most common schools of thought discussed in the realm of the ethics of image alteration and dissemination are *Utilitarianism* and Immanuel Kant's *Categorical Imperative*. The Categorical Imperative takes an absolutist approach to actions, categorizing them as either moral or immoral without consideration for context or motivation. For example, if a mother stole a piece of stale bread from a bakery because she had no money and her child was hungry, under the categorical imperative, this act would be wrong, because all stealing is immoral. On the other hand, a utilitarian assessment would factor in the dire circumstances of the mother and the fact that the bakery should not have tried to sell the stale bread.

Applying a utilitarian ethical evaluation is not always as clear as the previous example, however. To understand more clearly the dilemma of applying utilitarianism, consider the recently ended television series, *Breaking Bad*. It appears as though the creators of this series delight in pushing the audience's ability to rationalize the bad behavior of the lead character. The storyline of *Breaking Bad* revolves around the main character, Walter White, who is a high school chemistry teacher, dying of inoperable lung cancer. He decides to use his knowledge of chemistry to manufacture and distribute methamphetamine to provide for his family after his death. As the series progresses Walter finds himself in a series of situations where he is battling with the drug underworld and engages in murder and other nefarious activities in order to survive. As a result of his struggle with evil drug kingpins, he himself takes on the role of kingpin. Assuming you are able to rationalize Walter's initial behavior, at what point does utilitarianism judge his behavior to be unethical? Thus, applying utilitarianism consistently can be challenging.

Another ethical school of thought that is appropriate to images is hedonism. Ethical hedonism views pleasure as the ultimate good. In the context of images, pleasure can be interpreted as beauty, so under a hedonistic viewpoint an image is assessed for its beauty and nothing else. So, if an image of a beautiful woman is selected, no consideration is made as to whether she is being stereotyped as a sex object, for example.

The above ethical perspectives can be applied to specific images in context of a website, but we need additional guiding principles of correct behavior to complete our treatment of the ethics of image selection and alteration. The next section looks at the ethical guidelines for photojournalists as a reference point for good practice.

Principles of Professional Ethics

The professional field most closely associated with web development is photojournalism, because the dissemination of images to a wide audience is a central activity in both professions. So, using the code of ethics from National Press Photographers Association is a useful starting point. The code of ethics consists of nine points, some of which pertain to general professional ethics. The principles can be summed up as follows (NPPA, 2012):

1. Create accurate and complete representation of subjects.
2. Do not use staged photo opportunities.
3. Do not stereotype your subjects, and leave your own biases out of the work.
4. Treat subjects of your photography with respect, and be particularly sensitive to vulnerable individuals such as victims of crime or other tragedy. Also, be aware of the privacy needs for individuals who are grieving.
5. Be careful that in the act of recording an event, you do not become part of the event or alter the course of the event.

6. When editing photographs make sure you do not mislead viewers by misrepresenting the context or subjects of the photograph.
7. Do not pay subjects or sources.
8. Do not accept gifts or compensation from those who might wish to influence coverage of a topic.
9. Do not interfere with the work of other journalists.

One of the most important ethical considerations from the above list is to avoid misrepresenting reality, to the extent an image is intended to communicate a real event or situation. Additional considerations that pertain to selecting content for websites included avoiding the gratuitous portrayal of gore or violence and protecting the privacy of individuals beyond those who are grieving, as stipulated in item number four, above. If an individual is not a celebrity or a political figure, that person has a right to privacy. If you wish to include family, friends, acquaintances, or even strangers on your website, you should ask their permission first.

In order to better understand the challenge of applying ethical principles we will look at how various news sources chose to portray a newsworthy but gory scene next.

Ethical Case Study

An interesting exploration of the question of the portrayal of gore and the victims of violence can be made in the context of the 2013 Boston Marathon bombing. The New York newspaper, *The Daily News* was found to have edited a front page photo containing a bombing victim whose wounds were edited to appear to be covered by her pants (Haughney, 2013 and Pompeo, 2013). The primary ethical concern was that *The Daily News* was misrepresenting the bombing scene by editing out an injury. The newspaper was apparently attempting to avoid showing excessive gore, out of respect to the victim and her family and friends. Other news organizations also showed bombing scenes, but they cropped out more graphic injuries.

The Atlantic, on the other hand, chose to post an image on its website that contains explicit injuries (Haughey 2013,). The editorial board of *The Atlantic* defended this decision by claiming it was presenting the bombing incident in a realistic light. One might ask if it is ever good to show the gore that results from violence. On the other hand, can the systemic sanitizing of violence have a negative influence on society?

In the ethical evaluation of the portrayal of violence, it is beneficial to use a utilitarian approach. The portrayal of violence has definite negative elements. Victims and their loved ones should not be exposed to images in the media of their personal tragedy. Children should also not be exposed to such displays without parental guidance. So, one could rationalize that the systemic avoidance of violence is good for society. However, if one never witnesses the brutality of a terrorist attack or the horrors of war, a society may become complacent to such situations.

To better understand how the lack of exposure to images of the consequences of violence may lead to complacency, consider the difference between society's reaction to the Vietnam War and the war on Iraq, as initiated under President George W. Bush. The Vietnam War had more explicit coverage of the brutality of war, whereas the Iraq war presented little of the gore of war. As a result, American society opposed the Vietnam War earlier than the Iraq War. So, the portrayal of the consequences of violent, news-worthy acts is complex.

Other Examples of Image Editing in the Media

An excellent resource for finding well-known images that have been altered is a website called *famouspictures.org*, created by Dean Lucas. Although this website contains a wide range of iconic images, it has a separate category for altered images. Some of the altered images are famous because of their intention to hoax the public, like the 9/11 tourist who appears to have had his picture taken moments before a plane crashes into the first of the Twin Towers. These images are clear ethical violations. What are of more interest are the images that engage in smaller-scale alterations, without intending to perpetrate a hoax.

One of the images at the famouspictures.org site is of Katie Couric, a former television network news anchor. This image has been altered so that she appears to be thinner than she really was at the time. One could argue this from a hedonistic standpoint that the image was made to be more attractive to the viewer, and so should be considered a beneficial alteration. A utilitarian evaluation comes to a different conclusion, however. When the systemic thinning of women occurs in the media, and when there are too few examples of role models that have a more average or heavy-set body type, this can cause women and girls to feel that they deviate from the norm. Such dissatisfaction with one's body image may lead to harmful behaviors like eating disorders or feelings of inadequacy. Consequently, it is more important to portray individuals realistically in the media than to portray some notion of beauty by editing images.

There is also an image in which Nicolas Sarkozy has a bulge around his mid-section removed. This could be analyzed in a similar manner to the Katie Couric image. In the media there are more men that have average or heavy body types than there are women. If men are portrayed as sex objects, they are more apt to have exaggerated muscles than to be portrayed as thin. One could analyze the Sarkozy image edit in a similar manner as the Katie Couric image edit.

Another disturbing image alteration that appears at the *famouspictures.org* site involves the *Time Magazine* cover portraying O.J. Simpson. The original mug shot of O.J. Simpson used for the cover was significantly darkened. This alteration can be interpreted as playing on racial stereotypes by darkening his skin color in an attempt to make him appear sinister. The image edit could also suggest editorial bias in which the editorial board's opinion that O.J. Simpson was guilty of murdering Nicole Brown Simpson was expressed through the image modification. In any ethical analysis of this situation, it is difficult to determine any positive consequence of darkening the image. The darkening of the image was a professionally unacceptable practice.

As we can see, ethically questionable, image alterations occur in the mass media. In our web development we will not intentionally violate professional or ethical standards. Now that we've explored important ethical considerations, we can investigate tools one can use to alter images.

TOOLS FOR IMAGE EDITING

There are many choices for image-editing software. This section will highlight areas of functionality provided by higher-end image editing software. We will explore two examples of such software. One is a commercial product, Adobe Photoshop, while the other, GIMP, is available at no cost. Figure 5.6 shows the GIMP interface, featuring its tools, filter options, and layer dialog. In order to understand this class of image editing software, the common features of each product will be explored briefly.

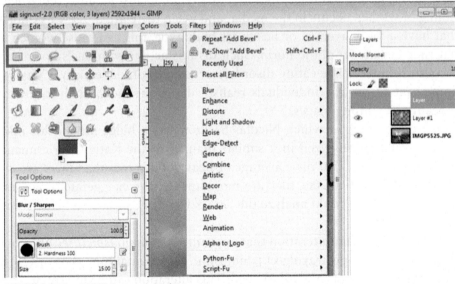

FIGURE 5.6 The GIMP image interface

Source: The GIMP Development Team.

Layers

One very powerful, yet at times confusing, feature of these image editors is that they maintain an image as distinct layers that can be combined at the discretion of the person editing the image. Layers enhance the flexibility of image editing. Consider for a moment an editing situation in which you edit the image of one person's head onto the image of another person's body. Without layers the head, would replace a certain amount of the background, making adjustments like rotating and resizing difficult. Also, if the skin tone needs adjustment, it would be difficult to control color adjustment so that it changes only the head. So, layers greatly improve image editing flexibility by isolating area for editing.

In order to maintain the separate layer definitions it is important to save the image editing project file. For Photoshop, the project file extension is .psd, while in GIMP the file extension is .xcf. The project files cannot be added to a web page, however. Both image editors allow the creation of image files from the project file. So, PNG, GIF, or JPEG images can be created by either application.

Precision Selection and Editing Tools

Another characteristic of advanced image editors is that they provide sophisticated selection tools. That is, they allow the ability to select areas of an image other than rectangles or ovals. A selection tool may select a specified color region with an adjustable color tolerance, or assist in edge detection when tracing the outline of an object. By precisely copying areas from one or more images and then combining them, one can create interesting image compositions to enhance one's website. The compositions might be serious or humorous in nature, or facilitate the creation of an image map, which will be the subject of the upcoming assignment. An image map is a web page embedded image that contains hotspots that serve as links to external websites, other pages within your website, or other regions on a web page.

Advanced image editors generally provide tools that facilitate the integration of multiple images. Certain adjustments may be necessary to make the combination of multiple images appear seamless. That is, the edges of the images being combined may not seem like they go together, so there are tools, like the smudge tool, that allow colors to be mixed. Other editing tools like a clone stamp allow copying an area of an image to another area of the same image. A clone stamp tool could be used to remove someone from a photo by copying background over the person to be removed. Other integration tools, like the burn and dodge tool, exit as well. The burn tool subtly lightens areas in an image, while the dodge tool darkens selected ares.

Textures, Filters, and Color Adjustments

Many advanced image editors provided a set of predefined patterns that can be used to enhance images. Some patterns simulate textures of common materials like wood, metal, plastic or cloth. Filters are another common feature of such image editors. Filters allow special effects to be applied to an image, such as lighting, a variety of distortions and effects that create a stylized look to an image, and transforming a photograph into what looks like an oil painting. One could use the liquefy tool to alter the expression on the image of a person's face to change their mood, for example. These editors also allow the adjustment of colors, contrast, and brightness.

This brief enumeration of image editor features just scratches the surface. One cannot learn image editing by reading a book. One must tackle a set of projects in order to gain proficiency with image editing. The next section provides a project to start the familiarization process.

CREATING AN IMAGE COMPOSITION/IMAGE MAP

The next step in advancing the website content is to create an image map for the purpose of navigating the website. This allows the creation of a larger-scale image to serve as the focal point of the main web page. It simplifies the content of the main page and draws the viewer into the website. This project will occur in two phases. The first phase involves the creation of the image composition using GIMP. The second phase is the creation of the image map using Amaya. An image map defines a set of hotspots on an image that serve as links. In this case we wish to link to pages in our website.

Creating the Image Composition with GIMP

Our goal for the image composition is to place graphic objects that relate to topics addressed by the website in a suitable context. For the hiking in the White Mountains website it makes sense to use White Mountain scenery for the context. Because the site will structure the content of the website around certain regions within the White Mountains, a sign will be created to contain those navigational hotspots. Because an additional content area discussing hiking equipment is planned for the website, a backpack will be edited into the composition.

Like most sophisticated image editing software, GIMP can take some time to become familiar with. One key to success when using GIMP is to be mindful of the layers that are created. When editing aspects of the image, make sure that you are on the correct layer. You may also find it useful to merge layers on occasion. This can be done by right-clicking on a layer and then selecting "merge down" or other suitable option from the menu.

Another consideration when using GIMP is that its strength is image editing rather than image creation. As a result, GIMP does not offer shape drawing tools like Adobe Photoshop does. It does, however, have basic shape selection tools, that can be used to select rectangular, oval, or hand-specified shapes that can be filled in with color or patterns by using the paint bucket tool.

This next section is not meant to serve as a tutorial, but rather to point the reader in the right direction for using GIMP. GIMP provides excellent tutorial instructions at its website, gimp.org.

The Basic Steps for Creating an Image Composition

Planning your image composition is the first critical step. Determine what you wish to use as your background and then find the elements you wish to edit into the background. Your background may need some adjustments as well to remove distracting elements. When you have saved your image resources into a suitable folder, you are ready to begin editing.

1. Open all relevant files in GIMP, using the menu options *file → open*. Each file should appear as an icon above the image editing area.
2. Use precision selection tools to extract the desired graphic objects from the open files.

    a. Click on the icon for the desired file.
    b. Use a selection tool, like the "scissors select tool," shown as a scissors icon in the tools menu. Use the selection tool to trace the desired object. You may need to drag your cursor on the selected object to complete the selection.
    c. Copy the selected object by selecting the menu options *edit → copy*.
    d. Select the background image by clicking on its icon.
    e. Paste the object onto the background image by selecting the menu options *edit → paste*.
    f. After you paste the object onto the background image, GIMP creates a "floating selection" in the "Layers" dialog. You may right click on this entry and specify "to new layer" to complete the paste operation.
    g. You will likely need to move, resize, add perspective, and/or rotate the object it to fit it into the composition properly. The tools shown below will help carry this out. By hovering the cursor over a tool's icon, GIMP shows the name and function of that tool.
    h. Save your GIMP project file early and often. The file extension for GIMP projects is .xcf.

3. Repeat step number two to copy and position each object.
4. You may wish to add text, using the text tool, which has the letter "A" as its icon in the tool menu. For example, Figure 5.7 illustrates the use of text in the construction of the sign pointing to regions of the White Mountains.
5. In order to integrate your objects better into your image composition, you may wish to explore the file options.

FIGURE 5.7 Image composition for the image map

6.   The clone tool (stamp icon) can be useful to edit out unwanted elements from your background image. Make sure the dimensions of your image composition are not too large. If so, resize the image to the approximate dimensions you anticipate using on your website.

7.   When you have copied and arranged your objects to your satisfaction, you are ready to export your image by using the menu options *File → export*. Use this export dialog to place your image in a web accessible folder and to determine the file type.

Once your image composition is complete, it can be transformed into an image map.

Creating an Image Map with Amaya

Amaya allows us to define hotspots on an image that will serve as hyperlinks. For our project, we wish to link to other web pages within our website from our main page or another web page in our site. Figure 5.8 shows how hotspots look in Amaya. When the web page is viewed using a regular web browser, the hot spots are invisible. In order to create an image map:

FIGURE 5.8 Tools to move, resize, add perspective, and/or rotate

Source: The GIMP Development Team.

1.   Insert an image in a web page.

2.   Insert a set of hot spots by selecting the main menu option *Insert → Map area → Rectangle area* or *Circle area* or *Polygon area.*

3.   Specify the URL that is to be associated with the hot spot in the pop-up dialog, as shown below.

Note that the link specified in the above dialog is a file name as

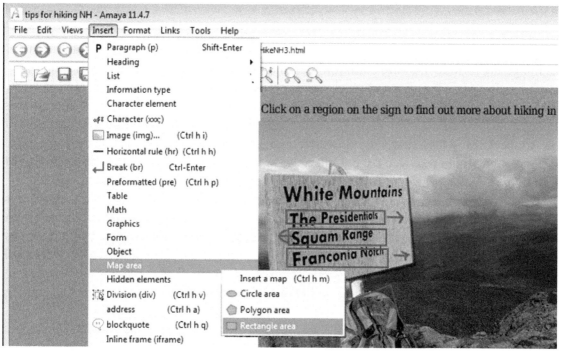

FIGURE 5.9 Creating hot spots on an image map

Source: W3C / INRIA.

FIGURE 5.10 Adding a link in Amaya

Source: W3C / INRIA.

opposed to a normal URL. This is because the file is part of the website and is stored in the same folder as the referencing web page (the main page in this case).

SUMMARY

Computers represent everything numerically, including images. There are a small number of image-file formats that are commonly used on the web. These are JPEG, GIF, and PNG. Each has its own strengths and weaknesses, so as web developers it is important to know which type of image format is best suited for our needs. Another important consideration is image size. Even though one may resize an image using a web page editing tool like Amaya or Adobe Dreamweaver, we should resize images to their approximate size on the page before adding them to a web page. Otherwise, if the image file is very large, independent of its size on the web page, its transmission over the Internet will be unnecessarily slow.

As we create, select or edit images using tools like GIMP and Adobe Photoshop, it is important to look at certain ethical considerations. The list of professional ethics rules put forward by the National Press Photographers Association is a good starting point. Some of the most important rules of ethics to take into account when developing web content are to make sure content does not to misrepresent reality, to avoid perpetuating stereotypes, to protect the privacy of others, and to and take care in presenting sensitive material, such as crime scenes.

High-end image editing tools, like GIMP and Adobe Photoshop, allow us to create sophisticated image compositions that can serve as image maps or other focal points on a web page. An image map is an image that has hot spots that link to other webpages or to other locations on a web page.

REFERENCES

Haughney, C.(2013 April 17). News media weigh use of photos of carnage. *The New York Times*. Retrieved from http://www.nytimes.com/2013/04/18/business/media/news-media-weigh-use-of-photos-of-carnage.html. B1.

NPPA (2012). NPPA Code of Ethics. Retrieved September 21, 2013 from https://nppa.org/code_of_ethics.

Pompeo, J. (2013 April 17). '*Daily News*' doctored front-page photo from Boston bombing. Retrieved September 21, 2013 from http://www.capitalnewyork.com/article/media/2013/04/8529102/daily-news-doctored-front-page-photo-boston-bombing.

CHAPTER SIX

WEBSITE DESIGN

POINTS TO CONSIDER

- What decisions does one make during website design?
- What does a modular design approach mean?
- Which aspects of design are addressed in this textbook?
- What decisions does one make during content design?
- What are three common website structures, and what type of web content would be suitable for each?

- Which website structure will your website embody?
- What is a site diagram?
- Draw the site diagram for your website.
- What decisions does one make during web page design?
- What is the look-and-feel of a website?
- What is an iframe?
- What design objectives do iframes help accomplish?
- What problems exist with using iframes?

INTRODUCTION

n order to create a website that is appealing to viewers and is easy to understand and use, good design is critical. There are two larger categories of design that will be addressed here. The first category of design entails how the information is structured in the website. This design area answers questions like, "how many web pages are there?", "how does one web page relate to the others?", and "what content goes in each page?" The other design category addresses the look-and-feel of the various web pages comprising a site. Design concerns addressed by this category include aesthetic appeal, readability, and consistency of design. We will explore the category of information and structural design first and refer to this topic as *content design*.

CONTENT DESIGN

The first step in content design is to determine the objectives of the web site. The process for establishing the goals of any software application is called analysis and is beyond the scope of this text. We will presume that the goals for this the website are self-evident, which may not always be the case. In this phase of design, the website goals should be related to content only. For example, a design goal of having an aesthetically pleasing site does not relate to the information contained in our website. Aesthetics are an important design concern, but they belong in our second category of design. An example of a content design goal for our sample hiking website could be "to inform people of the best hiking trails in the White Mountains."

The Question of Audience

Another concern that falls into the category of analysis is that of audience. Who do you anticipate visiting your website, or who do you wish to attract to your website? Are you developing web content for English speakers living in the U.S., or do you wish to reach out to an international audience? Is there a cultural aspect to your content? Do you wish to inform adults, children, teenagers, older individuals, or some combination of these groups? Is there special consideration for individuals with disabilities? The answer to these questions can influence the nature of the content, as well as the design of your site. As you are making content and design choices, it is important to keep your audience in mind.

The process of analyzing the objectives of a website, including the intended audience, can be expansive, but is beyond the goal of this textbook. We will instead launch into more the more concrete topic of design by establishing our organizing principles.

Organizing Principles

A website that lists all the information about White Mountain hikes as a single, expansive web page would be overwhelming and would not be considered a well-designed website. So, in order to continue our design process we need to establish a means to organize this large volume of information. In this case there are a number of possibilities. The hikes could be arranged by difficulty levels, with one page listing easy hikes, another listing moderate hikes, and a final page listing challenging hikes. A second organizational strategy could be to list hikes by geographic region. Since the White Mountains have previously established regions, these could serve as our organizing principle. Another possible organizing strategy is chronological. The hikes could be presented in order that they were hiked by the website developers.

In addition to the decision concerning which organizing strategy to select, another structural decision concerns how much information should be allotted to a single web page.

As was alluded to in chapter two, a modular approach to website design is advisable for beginning web developers, because a modular approach is easy to understand and results in a well-organized website. This means that a web page should contain the amount of information that would fit into the typical web browser window. This avoids the need to scroll to find information on the website and reduces the likelihood that a visitor to the website will miss vital information. What fits into a web browser window varies depending on window size and computer monitor resolution, so this measurement is approximate.

Because a visitor to the website is not likely to be interested in the sequence in which the web developers experienced the hikes listed at the website, a chronological organizing scheme is not advisable. A chronological approach is embodied by most weblogs, and this website is not meant to be a weblog. Either of the other two options could appeal to a visitor. In fact, a combination of the two could serve as a good organizing strategy. Hikes could be first organized geographically by region, and then within a region, the hikes could be further organized by difficulty. Alternatively, the hikes could be first organized by difficulty and then within a difficulty level the hikes could be organized geographically.

Both of the organizational strategies have appealing characteristics. A hiker looking for a specific difficulty level who is willing to travel to any area in the White Mountains would appreciate an organizational scheme that first organizes difficulty level. On the other hand, someone planning to visit a specific location within the White Mountains would favor the geographically oriented organizational approach.

This approach to information organization generally leads to a hierarchical website structure. The next section elaborates on three basic website structures.

WEBSITE STRUCTURE

Website structure refers to the intended sequence of web pages that web developers expect visitors to navigate. Figure 6.1 shows the hierarchical information breakdown of the hiking website. Such a hierarchical breakdown naturally translates into a hierarchical website structure by devoting a web page to each box in the diagram. The box at the top of the hierarchy would introduce viewers of the site to general information about hiking in the White Mountains and what kind of information to anticipate should they chose to explore the site further. From this page, the viewer could find additional information about the selected regions of the White Mountains. Each regional page would then list a series of hikes grouped by their difficulty level. At this point the website developers could decide whether to create web pages dedicated to difficulty level for each region or to simply link each regional page directly to hikes, classifying each hike according to difficulty.

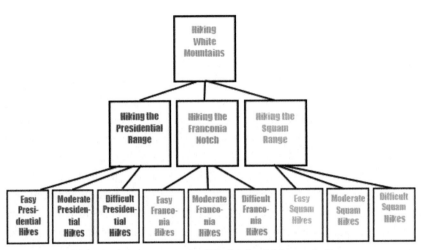

FIGURE 6.1 Sample information organization for the hiking website

Site Diagrams

A site diagram is a means to express the basic structure of a website, such as the hierarchical structure, just discussed. The goal of a site diagram is to represent a website as interrelated web pages. The diagram expresses the primary navigational sequences intended by the website developers. It is important to distinguish between the intended navigational sequence and web page links. Websites are often more fully linked than what is represented in a site diagram. The additional links allow for more flexibility of use. The layout of each web page should encourage visitors to use links specified in the site diagram, but should also provide additional links for navigational flexibility.

There are three common website structures, hierarchical, linear, and network. Although many sites are likely to use a combination of structures, most still reflect one of the three aforementioned structures as their predominant site layout. Figure 6.2 illustrates these common website structures. A hierarchical site structure is useful for novice visitors because navigation is relatively simple, as a result of having fewer navigational choices than the network structure. A network structure is useful for expert-level visitors because the flexibility of navigation could be confusing to someone less familiar with the content. A linear structure is extremely simple from a navigation standpoint, but its lack of flexibility limits its application.

We have seen an example of a hierarchical site structure through the hiking website. Many subject areas are suitable for such a website structure, because thinking about topics in their most general form and then progressively providing increased detail is a relatively easy-to-understand approach. A linear website layout is useful for information that

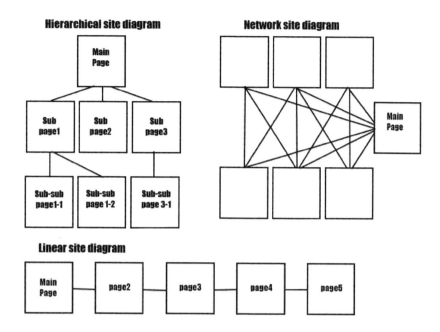

FIGURE 6.2 Three basic website structures

should be accessed sequentially, like a tutorial. A network site structure is suitable for sites in which the sequence of information is flexible. This type of website layout can be confusing for novices who may not know where to go first. This is also why in Figure 6.2 the web pages are not named/numbered with the exception of the main page. A network structure is best suited to experts who understand how to carry out their task. An example of a network structured website could be one where experts configure their avatar for a web-based game.

So far our discussion of website design has addressed the consideration of how web pages relate to each other. Another important consideration is the layout of an individual web page.

WEB PAGE DESIGN: STRUCTURAL CONSIDERATIONS

Interface design is a complex topic. Entire courses can be devoted to the question of interface design, so a comprehensive treatment of this question is beyond the scope of this text. We will instead present useful guidelines for beginning web developers. Our initial web page design concern will involve page structure, which establishes what information to select and where to place it on the web page.

One of our guiding design principles has been modularity. That is, each web page should be approximately the size of a web browser window and require minimal scrolling. Because each web page is therefore relatively small, we must use this space efficiently, and yet not be overly cluttered or complex.

The Main Page: Information Layout

The main page is the page that visitors to the website are intended to reach first. With the advent of web search engines, we are not guaranteed that visitors to our site will find our main page first, so good navigation from our subpages is critical. In order to keep our design process as simple as possible, we will proceed with the assumption that visitors to the site will start at the main page.

The main page should serve as a general introduction to the website, informing people of the content of the site and guiding them to more detailed information in the site's subpages. Additionally, the main page should be visually inviting and simple, so as to avoid overwhelming the viewer. Finally, the main page establishes the site's look-and-feel. That is, the rest of the website should have the same colors and share certain graphics so that the visitor understands that he or she has not linked to an external site. The focus of our design will start with information layout and then proceed to concerns of aesthetics.

The information elements that comprise the main page are title, navigation, graphics, and introductory information. One approach to designing the main page for our sample website is to create an image map, as we did in the previous chapter, in Figure 5.7. This provides a visually engaging central image, along with navigation to subpages of the site. There are essentially two problems with using this approach. The first is that image maps are not well suited for use by visually impaired people. The second problem is that being able to use the same navigational mechanism on the subpages is a good design approach, and repeating this large graphic on other pages wastes too much valuable space.

A better design approach entails using more traditional navigation tools like a menu or list of links. Figure 6.3 illustrates a very simple approach to designing the main page that uses a table to format the main page and a title image that combines the heading with a feature image along the top of the page. The table includes a column of linkable images that provide navigation to the subpages. The subpages contain information on hiking in the regions of the White Mountains and provide safety information. The central area contains text that welcomes the visitor to the website and describes very briefly what someone can expect from the website.

In addition to determining how web pages link to each other and what information to add and where it is placed on each page, there is another category of design consideration for web developers, namely aesthetics.

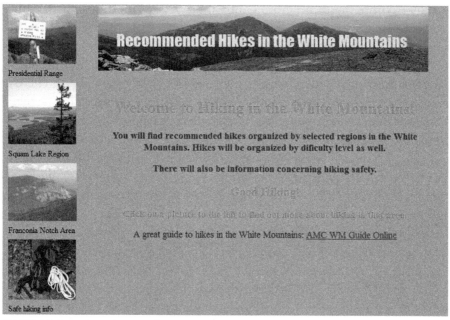

FIGURE 6.3 Sample main page for the hiking website

WEB PAGE DESIGN: AESTHETICS

Web page aesthetics involves decisions pertaining to color, font style and size, and image selection and size. The decisions made in this category should support our comprehensive design objectives, as follows:

- visual appeal and engagement;
- efficient use of space;
- minimal scrolling (modular design);
- good balance of text and images or other media;
- good readability and clear content;
- web page coherency;
- thematically and audience appropriate color choice;
- easy navigation; and
- layout and design (look-and-feel) consistency.

The question of aesthetics can be highly subjective and change significantly depending on the anticipated audience. For example, the color choices for the hiking website would be very different if we were trying to reach a child audience between the ages of seven to ten. The website would contain thematically appropriate earth tones for an adult audience, whereas brighter colors might be more captivating for a child audience. People who differ culturally may also associate colors with various themes differently. For example, the western sensibility of using white as a predominant color for a wedding website would not be appropriate for a Chinese wedding website, where red would be more suitable.

Cultural considerations aside, our websites need to draw in viewers. The overwhelming volume of content on the web allows viewers who are not visually engaged with our website many alternatives. Having visually attractive images as a centerpiece of our web page is a good strategy for accomplishing this. Because of our modular design approach, which limits the amount of content per page, it is important to ensure that our images not only are attractive but also informative. Figure 6.3 illustrates this principle in the header, which combines a photo of the White Mountains with the title of the website. In order to further use space effectively on each page, tables are critical so that the horizontal area of each web page can be effectively used.

Clear and readable content is critical. Background and font color must have good contrast, but not be garish. Font choices are somewhat limited, because the viewer of our website will see fonts that are installed on the local machine, rather than the website server. When a web page is downloaded, the fonts are not transmitted. If you want the viewer's experience to be similar to the one you create, then using relatively standard fonts is advisable. This explains why Amaya and Adobe Dreamweaver offer a limited choice when it comes to fonts.

Web page coherency addresses the meaning of the content. A coherently designed web page has a clear purpose for its content. All of the content on a coherent page should address the page's purpose, with the exception of navigational mechanisms. Navigational mechanisms should be clear, consistent, and easy to use. The final design principle, layout and design consistency, is addressed in the next section, as look-and-feel.

Establishing the Website's Look-and-Feel: Frames and Cascading Style Sheets

A website should embody a design consistency that communicates to the visitor that they are at your site, rather clicking a link that brings them to a different website. The elements that may comprise a website's look-and-feel include color scheme, navigation mechanism, headings, graphics, spacing, and logos. The color scheme includes text and background colors or images. There are mechanisms that help web developers apply a consistent design to multiple web pages. There are two main complementary approaches to this objective: frames and cascading style sheets (CSS). Cascading style sheets will be covered in the chapter on advanced design and accessibility.

Frames are a mechanism that allows a web page to be divided into distinct addressable areas. This facilitates consistency in look-and-feel by allowing certain areas of the web page to remain the same, while other areas change in response to visitor activity, such as clicking on links. For example, the web page in Figure 6.3 has a column of linkable thumbnail

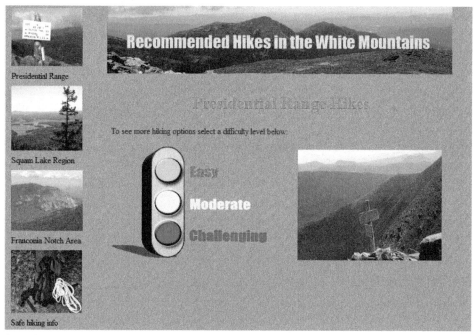

FIGURE 6.4 View of hiking website after the "Presidential Range" thumbnail is clicked on

images as a frame that remains unchanged, while the central area of the web page changes depending on which link the visitor clicks on. The image shown in Figure 6.4 is the result of someone clicking on the "Presidential Range" thumbnail. Only the middle area of the web page is updated, thus retaining the look-and-feel of the website, including the standard navigation mechanism.

With the exception of iframes, frames are not supported in Amaya. According to the Amaya FAQ, frames create problems with how the web should function, due to creating unpredictable results when the web browser back button is clicked, complicating the determination of URLs, and complicating use by people with visual disabilities (Vatton 2012). The reason URLs are complicated by the use of frames is because the URL of a specific hike is the same as the main website. This is because the hike information appears in the iframe area of the web page, so the URL of the page does not change. So, if someone wishes to advise people to investigate a specific hike, there is no URL available to direct people to this hike. At best, people can be sent the URL for the site and given direction about which region and difficulty level the hike is filed under. So, frames do present a significant weakness.

The negative consequences of using frames are balanced by the benefits of avoiding redundant information in web pages. One frames-free way to replicate navigation structures like tables of thumbnails linking to topics within a website, like in Figure 6.4, is to copy this table onto all the pages of the website. This would work initially, but if a new region of hiking is introduced to the website, and the navigation table changes, this would mean every web page would have to be modified, as opposed to modifying one web page, if one had used iframes.

Of course, other options exist to avoid redundant content on web pages and also avoid using frames. The problem is that these options are not suitable for beginning web developers. Such options entail using scripting languages to parse a URL which embodies an information request beyond the location of a web page. For example, if one wishes to send a friend a page of cute cat videos from a Google.com search, the URL would be https://www.google.com/#q=cute+cat+videos. This URL identifies the URL of the search engine and encodes the search terms as part of the URL. Something similar could be done on the hiking website to specify a specific hike, but because this alternative requires programming in a scripting language, and is out of the scope of this text. So, we will provide an optional solution entailing the use of iframes in the sample exercise, for those who wish to avoid the redundancy of repeating navigational devices.

DESIGN EXAMPLE

Our goal for this phase in our website development is to improve the layout of our web pages and to provide a consistent look-and-feel for all web pages in the site. Tables will be used to structure information on each web page. A consistent navigation mechanism will be used on all web pages to help provide a consistent look-and-feel. As beginning web developers, you may choose to use iframes to reduce redundancy, or to copy the navigation mechanism unto the subpages. The how-to instructions will cover the use of iframes, but these steps may be skipped and replaced with copying and pasting the common elements from one web page to another.

Before altering the layout and contents of any web pages, it is a good idea to prepare any images to be used. In our illustration, a set of thumbnail images is necessary to support our navigational device. The header image, which combines the panorama of the White Mountains with the title of the website, should also be created.

Creating the Thumbnail Images

The creation of thumbnail images requires identifying images to serve as our thumbnails and scaling them to be smaller and saving them. Once the originals have been identified,

1. start GIMP and open each original;
2. Select the menu options *Image →Scale* image. The following dialog will pop up:

3. Specify a suitable width (or height), making sure that the dimensions are linked using the chain link icon, and press the *Scale* button at the bottom of the window. Linking the dimensions ensures that the image will not become distorted during resizing.

4. Export the smaller image as a suitable file type (.jpg, .gif or .png). Make sure you rename the thumbnail so that you do not lose your original image.

5. Store your files in a web-accessible directory.

FIGURE 6.5 Scale image window

Source: The GIMP Development Team.

Structuring the Web Page Layout

This example uses tables and iframes to create a consistent look-and-feel and navigation mechanism. Figure 6.6 shows the same web page as in Figure 6.3, with the exception that the table is hidden in Figure 6.3 and showing in Figure 6.6 The solution in both figures uses

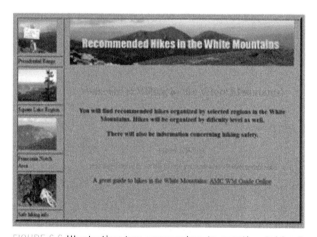
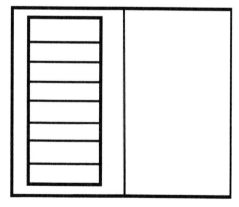

FIGURE 6.6 Illustrating two approaches to creating tables to structure web page content

a table with eight rows and two columns. The right column has been set up to contain a single cell that spans eight rows. Figure 6.6 shows an equivalent table structure using two tables, one nested inside the other. The outer table has a single row and two columns with the left column containing another table consisting of one column and eight rows.

To use a table as shown in Figure 6.6 using Amaya.

1. Open or create a new web page using the menu options *file → open* or *file → new*.
2. Add the table using the menu options *Insert → Table → Insert a table*. Using the table dialog, specify the number of rows and columns desired. Until the content has been placed in the table, the border of the table should be at least *one*. Otherwise it will be invisible. When the web page is complete the border can be updated to zero to hide the border.
3. In order to create one large cell on the right side of the table, select the top cell on the right side of the table by clicking in it. Then select the menu options, *Tools → Edit Table → Join with the cell below*, as shown in Figure 6.7. Repeat this step until the right cell takes up the entire right side of the table (six more times).
4. Place content in each cell on the left side of the table by clicking in that cell and inserting a thumbnail image (*Insert → Image*) and its caption.
5. On the right side of the table, insert the header image.

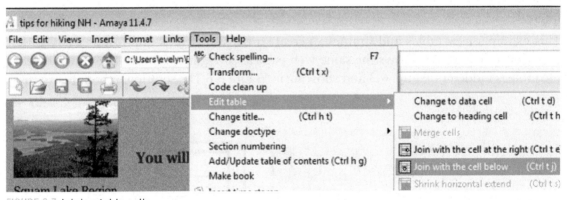

FIGURE 6.7 Joining table cells

Source: W3C / INRIA.

Preparing for the Inline Frame (Iframe)

Create a new web page that will contain the welcome information for your website. The welcome page for the hiking site is shown in Figure 6.8. Keep in mind that this page is intended to be a part of the main web page and will be surrounded by the thumbnail images and the header image. Additional subpages should also be prepared so that each thumbnail image has a page to link to.

Inserting the Inline Frame

The following instructions will add the iframe to the web page and redirect the pages that the thumbnail images are linked to so that they appear in the iframe.

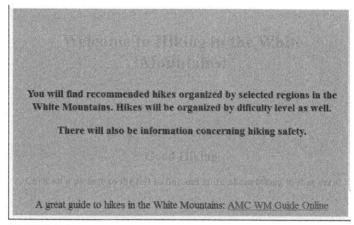

FIGURE 6.8 Iframe portion of welcome page

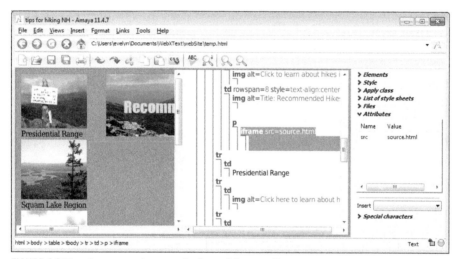

FIGURE 6.9 The Amaya environment after adding an iframe

Source: W3C / INRIA.

1. Place your cursor in the right side of the table under the header image and select the menu options, *Insert → Inline frame* (iframe).
2. The Amaya environment will respond to the previous step by opening a window containing HTML tag references, as shown in Figure 6.9. Click on the iframe reference in this new window to highlight this entry.

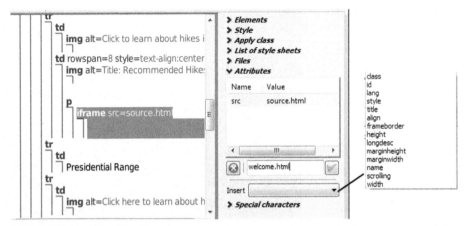

FIGURE 6.10 Updating the iframe

Source: W3C / INRIA.

3. In the rightmost portion of the Amaya window shown in Figure 6.9 is the tool dialog of the Amaya interface. Reveal the details of the attributes by clicking on the greater-than sign next to the *Attribute* label. Please note that the attributes may already be revealed.

4. The iframe references the web page *source.html* by default. Click on the entry *src source.html* in the attribute window, as shown in Figure 6.10, and change the entry from *source.html* to *welcome.html* (or your choice of web page) in the text field below the attribute window. Take care to spell the file name correctly.

5. Using the *Insert* pull-down box, additional attributes can be specified for the iframe. The attribute options available for the iframe are shown to the right of the Amaya interface in Figure 6.9. For

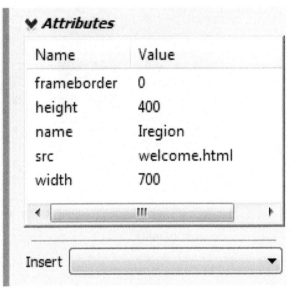

FIGURE 6.11 Recommended attribute values for the iframe

Source: W3C / INRIA.

example, to define a width for the iframe. Select *width* from the Insert pull-down menu and then, in the text field above the pull-down menu, enter the desired width. Click on the green arrow to complete this operation. Repeat this step for each desired attribute. Figure 6.11 shows sample values for recommended attributes. Please note that the *name* attribute is particularly important to allow hyperlinks to update the iframe with other web pages.

Targeting Hyperlinks to the Iframe

Now that the iframe has been added to the web page and assigned the name, *Iregion*, we are now able to influence the contents of the iframe depending on which thumbnail image is clicked on. In order to carry out this last step, we need to add a hyperlink to each thumbnail and then reference the iframe as the target for the hyperlinked web page.

1. Click on a thumbnail to add a link to a web page by selecting the menu options *Link → Create or change link*. Use the folder icon in the link dialog to select the desired web page.

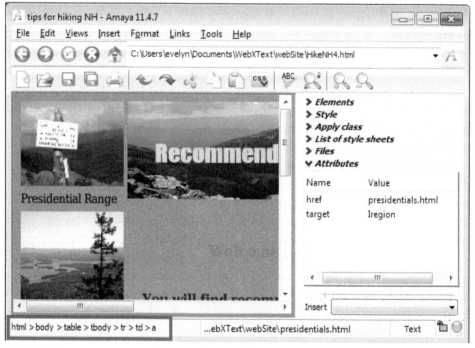

FIGURE 6.12 Adding the target to a link

Source: W3C / INRIA.

2. In order to specify the target (destination) of the linked to web page as the iframe, we need to add the *target* attribute to the link, rather than to the image. Press the *F2* button so that the attributes for the link appear in the attribute window, as shown in Figure 6.12. The attribute for a link is *href*. If you have difficulty specifying the link for attribute update, you can click on the letter "a" in the lower left of the Amaya interface. This area is indicated by a red rectangle in Figure 6.12. It is possible to simply click in this area to select an element for updating at any time.

3. Using the *Insert* drop-down menu select the attribute, *target,* and specify *Iregion* in the text field that opens up. Click on the green arrow to complete this operation.

4. Repeat steps 1 through 3 for each thumbnail image.

5. Save all your files to your web accessible directory.

6. Test your web page and make any necessary corrections.

SUMMARY

When engaging in real-world web development, determining the goals and audience for one's website is critical to its success. This determination is done in the analysis phase, which is beyond the scope of this text. Instead, this chapter presumes that the goals of our introductory websites are relatively self-evident and proceeds with the design phase of web development. This chapter addresses two aspects of design, namely *content design* and *web page design.* In content design one seeks a strategy to organize the information contained in the website. One guiding principle to design that has been recommended since chapter two is modularity. In a modular website, each web page addresses a clear content area and does not require excessive scrolling to view the content of a given page. A common modular website structure is a hierarchy, where one addresses the content generally at the top of the hierarchy and then breaks the topic down into progressively more detailed subtopics as one progresses down the hierarchy. Other website structures include linear and network.

Web page design addresses concerns about the aesthetics, navigation and look-and-feel of a website. Web pages that comprise a website should have a consistent layout, color scheme, and navigation mechanism. This consistency assures the viewer of the website that he or she has not been linked to another website, but is still at your website. An iframe is a means to create a consistent look-and-feel on a website and also avoid redundancy. There are problems with using an iframe; for example, the URL of desired content cannot be specified. There are ways to propagate a website's look-and-feel and avoid redundancy, but these means entail programming in a scripting language, which is beyond the scope of this textbook. One can use cascading style sheets (CSS), which will be addressed in a later chapter, to apply certain elements of design throughout a website.

REFERENCES

Vatton, I.(2012 October). Amaya Frequently Asked Questions. Retrieved June 29, 2014 from http://www.w3.org/Amaya/User/FAQ.html#II11.

CHAPTER SEVEN

ANIMATION

POINTS TO CONSIDER

- How are animations similar to flipbooks?
- How are animations similar to movies?
- What is raster graphics?
- What is vector graphics?
- What are the strengths and weaknesses of vector graphics versus raster graphics?
- Why are vector graphics particularly important in the context of creating animations?
- Describe the different ways may one approach creating animations.

- What common functionality does most animation software share?
- What are the strengths and weaknesses of Pencil?
- What are the strengths and weaknesses of Anime Studio?
- What are the strengths and weaknesses of Adobe Flash?
- What are some good ways to use animations on the web?

INTRODUCTION

When contemplating animations, we may think about a time when we were children and created a flipbook. For those who may have missed this opportunity, a flipbook is a notebook of blank sheets of paper in which we draw one or more basic figures. The figures are repeated on each page with minor variations in the drawing from one page to the next. When the series of pictures is complete, the animation is viewed by holding onto a corner of the notebook while allowing the pages to flip in rapid succession.

Figure 7.1 illustrates a simple flipbook scenario. This flipbook is rather brief, consisting of only six pages, but is useful to illustrate the basic concept of flipbooks. Each subsequent page embodies a small change from the previous page, so when shown in rapid succession, the figure appears to take a step. Movie films use the same principle as flipbooks. A movie film is a series of images that have small changes from one frame

FIGURE 7.1 Sample flipbook

FIGURE 7.2 Sample frame sequence showing a ball bouncing

to the next. These frames are shown in rapid succession to simulate motion to the viewer. Some types of animation resemble films in that they are a sequence of images with minor variation from one image to the next. Figure 7.2 shows a possible animated film consisting of eight frames depicting a ball bouncing into and then out of the frame.

There are a variety of types of animations. Cartoons are one familiar form of animation. Many may recall watching cartoons as children, like Looney Tunes or Walt Disney films.

There are also stop-motion animations like Wallace and Grommet. Stop-motion animation uses a still camera to create a sequence of images. A scene is usually set up and a camera is placed to capture the scene. Small changes are made to the scene between each picture. These pictures are then sequenced like a film to create the animation. Another category of animation is computer-generated animations. There are a variety of techniques by which one may use computers to generate animations. We will explore computer-generated animation in this chapter.

Animation is an important web-development topic, because it is a powerful means to connect with people. Animation can be used to get attention, to educate or simply to entertain. A significant decision to make when contemplating introducing animation onto a web site is which animation tool or computer language to use. If one wishes to create animations and not spend a large sum of money, then the choices can be challenging.

Before we discuss specific options for creating animations, we will explore general concepts pertaining to animation. Because images are a building block of animations, we will address basic options of image representation used by animation software first.

RASTER GRAPHICS VERSUS VECTOR GRAPHICS

Recall that in chapter five, the technical details of how images are stored on computers were discussed. This discussion addressed a category of images known as raster images, because these are the only image types currently supported by most web browsers. Many animation tools, however, use, to varying degrees, vector graphics, so it is important to understand this category of image.

Please recall the file types discussed in chapter five, PNG, JPEG, GIF and BMP. These file types are known as raster because an image of this type is represented as a collection of pixels of varying colors. In contrast, vector images are represented as a collection of geometric shapes. Each shape in a vector graphic image has an edge, dimension, location and color. As a result, vector graphics are best used for images that are not photorealistic. Figure 7.3 shows two versions of a segment of a waterfall image. The left side is a JPEG image, while the other shows what a vector version of the same might look like. Many of the nuanced colors that would naturally comprise the water, rocks, and vegetation are consolidated to allow for larger swaths of the same color. This consolidation of color tends to create a cartoonish effect.

FIGURE 7.3 A raster image on the left compared to a vector graphics version of the same image

Vector graphics have some benefits and some disadvantages when compared to raster graphics. Some disadvantages are as follows. They are

- not suited to photorealistic representation;
- not supported by most web browsers;
- possibly drawn differently when using different software; and
- possibly (depending on complexity) slower to be drawn.

On the other hand, there are important advantages to vector graphics when compared to raster graphics. These advantages are what make this form of image representation particularly attractive to animators. These advantages include the following. Vector graphics

- have small file sizes;
- are infinitely scalable, since the shapes can be drawn at any size without reduction in resolution;
- are easy to update with vector graphics software; and
- work well with line drawings.

As you might recall from chapter five, it is important to be aware of image file sizes and to strive to be as efficient as possible to avoid long download times. Since animations consist of multiple images, this concern for efficiency is compounded. This explains why vector graphics are so attractive to animators.

The advantages of vector graphics stem from their efficient approach to representing image information. To better understand this approach, we will explore a simple example in the next section.

SIMPLE VECTOR GRAPHICS EXAMPLE

In order to better appreciate the efficiency of vector graphics, Figure 7.4 will serve as a concrete example. The image in question is of a snowman. The numbers shown in the figure reflect dimensions and coordinates of the shapes comprising the image and are not intended to be part of the image. The image area for a vector graphic is defined by the rectangle surrounding the snowman. This rectangular image area defines a graphics coordinate area, which is used to identify where each shape should be placed. Each shape requires the following information:

- type of shape;
- location using x, y coordinates;
- dimensions;
- outer edge stroke type and color; and
- fill color.

Figure 7.4 shows the graphic coordinate system used to locate each shape comprising the image. The upper left-hand corner is (0, 0) and the lower right-hand corner identifies the maximum horizontal (x) and vertical (y) value in the image. Each image is located in this graphics coordinate space. For example, the upper rectangle making up the snowman's hat is located at (90, 0), which means that the beginning of the rectangle is 90 units to the right

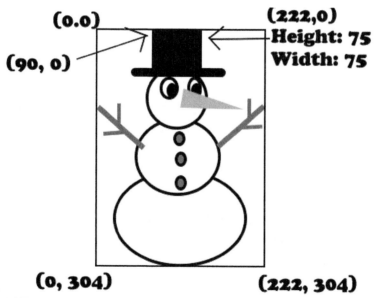

FIGURE 7.4 Example used to illustrate vector graphic image representation

of the left-most edge of the image and that it is at the upper edge of the image. The rectangle has a width and height of 75,
which makes it a square. The outer edge of the square is black, as is the fill color, so the outer edge is not visually distinct from the inside of the square. The outer edge is a solid line of one pixel.

The rest of the snowman is defined similarly to that of the square. The ovals making up the snowman's head and body require similar information as the square. In the case of the ovals, they have different colors used for the outer edge and the fill, to better illustrate the distinction between these elements of a shape.

The snowman consists of eight rectangles, ten ovals, and one polygon (triangle). This representation is very concise and results in very small file sizes. Because animations can have very large file sizes, the appeal of vector graphics is clear. A wide array of animation software exists, and each software tool varies in the role that vector graphics plays in that tool. The variation ranges from vector graphics playing no role to playing a central role.

The next section will briefly explore three approaches to animation to allow a deeper discussion of animation tools.

APPROACHES TO COMPUTER-BASED ANIMATION

When embarking on computer generated animation, there are three major approaches:
1. Stop motion
2. Computer Programming/Scripting language
3. Manual
   - Frame by frame specification
   - Periodic frame specification with automated transition calculation

Stop motion animation was previously compared to a flipbook because it entails showing a sequence of images in rapid succession. An animation tool that supports stop-motion animation should allow easy importing of photographic images, which are generally saved in JPEG format.

Animations can also be produced using computer programming or scripting languages. For example, web-based animations have been created with the computer programming language Java. HTML-5 compliant animations can be created using Javascript or Cascading Styles Sheets (CSS). Some animation tools have their own scripting language embedded in the tool. Adobe Flash and Anime Studio both have scripting languages. Adobe Flash uses ActionScript as its scripting language, while Anime Studio uses Lua.

Creating animations manually using an animation tool means that the animator speci-fies the placement of each animated object during the course of the animation, and then the tool creates a video that recreates the specified motion. One distinction between animation tools is whether the tool will interpolate the position of an object from one point to another over a period of time, or if the animator must specify the position of a graphic object for each frame.

The next section will introduce common elements found in most animation tools. Afterwards, three specific animation tools will be discussed.

COMMON ELEMENTS IN ANIMATION SOFTWARE

As previously mentioned, animation software varies greatly in the role that vector graphics plays. Despite this difference, animation software shares certain common characteristics. There are obvious commonalities that pertain to universal file functions such as saving project files and creating animation files of various formats. More interesting commonalities arise from the shared objective to allow animators to simulate creating a film-like sequence of frames. In order to accomplish this objective, animators need an area to define the contents of each frame. A means to navigate from one frame to another is also necessary. Finally, one needs tools with which to create content for each frame of the animated movie. Another common feature of most animation software is that content for each frame is organized into layers.

Figure 7.5 illustrates a generic animation tool interface. The drawing area is shown as the large rectangular area which contains the image of the mountains, stream, raccoon, and a person. The two columns of buttons along the right side of the interface represent a variety of drawing tools, such as a paintbrush, selection/manipulation tool(s), color selection tool, geometric shape tools, and eraser tool. The lower portion of the interface has a rectangular area, known as the timeline, containing a horizontal and vertical configuration of lines. The upper portion of this area is numbered in increments of five, while the left-hand side of the rectangle has a column of words naming the layers. Each column of the timeline represents one frame, which we can think of as a movie frame. The reason this collection of frames is called a timeline is that frames are played at some specified speed. For example, movies are played at a frame rate of twenty-four frames per second, so at this rate, twenty-four frames takes one second. Time can be measured in seconds on the timeline in increments of twenty-four frames.

The labels that run along the left-hand side of the timeline identify the layers comprising the animation. Most animation software requires each object that moves independently to be on its own layer. Graphic objects on each layer can be moved or modified gradually from frame to frame in order to simulate motion. Graphic objects can enter into the scene or leave the scene at any frame in the timeline. The timeline has some means of representing a change in position, size, or color of a graphic object. In Figure 7.5, these changes are

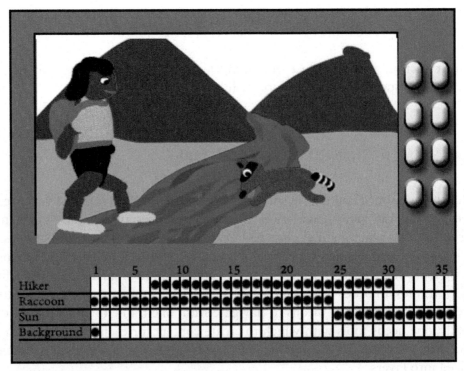

FIGURE 7.5 A sample generic animation tool

shown as dots in the timeline. For example, the timeline indicates that the hiker enters into the scene in the seventh frame and moves during each frame until the thirtieth frame, at which time it exits the stage. In contrast, the background is present in the first frame and does not change for the duration of the animation. The timeline indicates the lack of change in the background through the lack of dots.

Now that we have looked at the common elements unifying animation software, we can discuss individual examples. Three animation tools have been selected for discussion in the next section.

COMPARING ANIMATION TOOLS

A large number of free animation tools have been omitted from consideration for discussion here because they do not allow animators to save their animation files where they choose, or the tools do not produce a format suitable to embedding in web pages. The three tools to be discussed here have been selected because they are industry standards or are not excessively expensive and yet are reasonably powerful. Another criteria for consideration is that each tool treats vector graphics differently than the others do. One tool uses vector graphics heavily, another uses both vector graphics and raster graphics equally, and though the final tool uses raster and vector graphics, the power of vector graphics is not fully exploited. The animation tools to be discussed are the following:

- Pencil;
- Anime Studio; and
- Adobe Flash.

Pencil

Pencil is a freely available animation tool, and is self-described as "traditional animation software." The reason that it is considered traditional is that the primary mode of animation entails drawing a sequence of images with small variations between each image. This mode of animation is how early animators worked. Pencil is a computerized version of the early paper and pencil technique. Although Pencil allows animators to draw using vector graphics, vector graphics cannot be morphed, resized, or relocated, as they can be using other animation tools. Instead, each frame has to be redrawn in every frame.

Another important point to emphasize is that Pencil does not calculate object transitions in a multi-frame span. In other words, if an object is in a starting position in frame one and is moved significantly to another position in frame twenty, there is no means to have Pencil calculate a series of incremental changes in position so that the object moves smoothly between frames one and twenty. Both Adobe Flash and Anime

FIGURE 7.6 An animated figure walking in the woods

Studio allow for such calculation, so this point will be discussed in greater detail when these tools are addressed.

Another important capability that Pencil lacks is the ability to embed animations inside other animations. To illustrate the value of this capability, imagine an animated woodland scene in which a character walks down a path, as in Figure 7.6. If one could create a walking character by animating the walking motion once and letting the animation repeat the walking motion, the walking character could then be added to the woodland scene. By simply moving the walking character along the desired path in the woods, it would appear to walk along that path due to the repeated walking motion of the figure. If the walking character cannot be brought into the scene, the animator will have to animate the walking motion over and over as the character is moved through the scene. This can be an onerous task and difficult to pull off smoothly.

Although stop-motion animation is possible with Pencil, it is cumbersome. Pencil will not import JPEG files, which is the image format associated with photorealism. In order for images to be imported into Pencil, they must be either GIF or PNG format. Also, Pencil does not recognize image sequences to allow easy bulk imports. So, creating stop-motion animations with Pencil is a tedious process. A number of other features lacking in Pencil are object hierarchies and a scripting language.

Adobe Flash

Adobe Flash is the dominant tool for creating dynamic content for the web. This dominance has been challenged by the latest standard in HTML, HTML5. Adobe Flash exports .swf format animation files, which are not part of the new HTML standard. Adobe quickly responded to this change by adding .mov formatted videos to its list of export formats, so that Flash will be HTML5 compliant. However, when exporting an animation to a .mov format, Flash does not include any ActionScript-based motion or interactivity, so Adobe created Edge to facilitate the creation of ActionScript-based games and animations that are HTML5 compliant.

Adobe Flash is a commercial product, unlike Pencil, and carries a hefty price tag. As of the writing of this textbook, Flash can only be rented by the month as opposed to purchased. Over time, this can result in a significant investment. The positive side of having an expensive tool is that it provides sophisticated animation capability. One particularly useful capability is called *tweening*. Tweening allows the animator to specify a beginning position for a graphic object and an end point further down the timeline. Flash will calculate a frame by frame path for that object. The animator can then edit the path so that the object does not need to move in a straight line.

Another powerful capability provided by Flash is the ability to embed moving objects inside other animations. For example, in the Pencil discussion illustrated in Figure 7.6 where a walking figure is animated independently and then added to a forest scene, Flash allows the animator to animate a walking motion in the figure, which is then repeated. The walking figure can now be introduced into a scene where it moves along a path. The animator need only to specify the path that the figure should walk along without needing to address the walking motion once it has been introduced.

Another capability provided by Flash is the ability to create an object hierarchy. This concept is related to the previous topic of embedding animations inside other animations. What distinguishes object hierarchies from the embedding of animations is that with object hierarchies the animated elements are part of the larger object. Consider the ant pictured in Figure 7.7. The ant contains six leg objects. The animator can animate a single leg and replicate this leg five times. Because the legs are part of the ant, when the ant is moved along a path in the animation, the legs follow while repeating their leg motion.

Flash is also particularly good at facilitating stop-motion animations. As mentioned before, a stop-motion animation is composed of a large sequence of images. When importing images for such an animation, Flash recognizes that the images are part of a larger sequence, if they are named appropriately, and asks the animator if the entire sequence should be imported. For example, if one has a series of images named, image01.jpg, image02.jpg, image03.jpg, and so on, flash will recognize this as a sequence of images and ask the animator if all images in the sequence should be imported. Thus, once one has the desired images that will comprise the animation, it is relatively easy to create the animation using Flash.

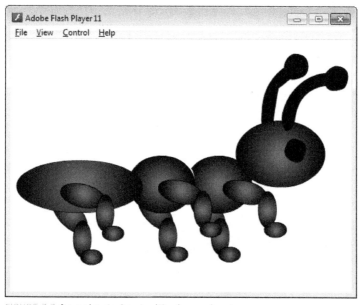

FIGURE 7.7 An animated ant with six moving legs

The real power of Flash lies in its scripting language, ActionScript. Animations can be created using ActionScript alone or by using a combination of manual and programmed animation. ActionScript also allows animations to be interactive. Thus, animations can be responsive to mouse movements and other user activity.

TABLE 7.1 Summary of key features of the animation tools

ANIMATION TOOL	EMBEDDING ANIMATIONS IN OTHER ANIMATIONS	ALLOWS CREATION OF STOP-MOTION ANIMATIONS	USE OF VECTOR GRAPHICS	TYPE OF EXPORT FORMATS	SCRIPTING LANGUAGE	OBJECT HIERARCHIES
Pencil	No	Limited	Limited	.swf .mov	None	No
Flash	Yes	Yes	Drawing tools create	.swf .mov	Action-Script	Yes
Anime Studio	No	Very brief segments only	Extensive	.mov .avi .swf	Lua	Yes

Finally, Flash provides a set of basic drawing tools that allow animators to create vector graphic objects. This allows animators to create simple graphic objects that can be animated rather than having to import all of the graphics. However, the drawing tools can be frustrating to work with if one is accustomed to working with image editing and drawing tools, like Adobe Photoshop.

Anime Studio

Anime Studio is structurally different from both Adobe Flash and Pencil. It is not free like Pencil, but is more affordable than Adobe Flash. It has an introductory version known *Debut* that is very affordable for students. Though the *Pro* version of the software is pricier than the Debut version, it is still reasonably affordable. Its strength lies in the features it provides that allow the creation of sophisticated characters. Anime Studio facilitates the creation of a hierarchy of layers, as opposed to a hierarchy of objects, like Adobe Flash. In Anime Studio, each layer in the hierarchy usually corresponds to a moving/changing component of a character. Anime Studio has six customizable layer types that also contribute to the definition of complex characters. Anime Studio also provides a character wizard and a library of predefined characters that can be customized. The process of modifying predefined characters facilitates learning character creation.

The six layer types provided by Anime Studio (Debut version) are:

- Vector—supports the creation and transformation of vector graphics
- Image—supports importing raster graphics
- Bone—supports the creation of sub layers (to form a layer hierarchy)

- Switch—supports the creation of sub layers, but only one layer can be active at a time.
- Audio—allow recording audio
- Text—allows the specification of the font, color, and size of text.

Two layer types are dedicated to containing graphic objects. The first of these layer types, vector, contains vector images and allows the animation of vector objects. Animators can specify the vertices of a vector object in one key frame and then specify new placements for the vertices of the object several frames down the timeline and allow Anime Studio to interpolate the intervening positions, much like Adobe Flash's tweening. The tweening-like interpolation that exists in Anime Studio is the norm for animating. That is, one does not need to take special action to activate the interpolation. Image layers are the second layer type that contains graphic objects. Image layers are similar to vector layers, except they contain raster images, rather than vector images. These layer types also allow the interpolation of image size and position between key frames.

Bone layers facilitate the creation of a hierarchy of layers by serving as a container for other layers. Because bone layers can contain other bone layers, a sophisticated hierarchy of components can be created, making it possible to develop complex characters. As the name implies, bone layers also allow the use of a bone tool to connect components of animated characters in a skeleton-like manner. This bone structure allows the creation of realistic movement, but can be difficult to use for beginning animators. Anime Studio provides a number of predefined characters that can be imported, so beginning animators can work with predefined bone structures before creating their own.

Another important layer type is the switch layer. The switch layer allows animators to define a sequence of image and/or vector layers, only one of which may be displayed at any given time. This allows for the creation of various facial expressions. For example, if a character talks, it can have a series of mouth images that correspond to forming specific syllables. The animator can then specify which mouth image should be shown during dialog to create realistic animated mouth motion.

The final two layer types, audio and text, allow the inclusion of audio and text respectively. These two layer types round out a set of powerful layer types comprising a sophisticated animation tool that is reasonably priced. In addition to the various layer types provided, animators have the ability to control a camera that determines the angle and size of the area shown in the final exported video.

Having surveyed a representative set of animation tools and looked at their features, we are now ready to contemplate how to harness this capability for the web. We will explore how animations can be used on the Web in the next section.

USING ANIMATIONS ON THE WEB

There is much interactivity on the Web that one might classify as animation, but creating animations that respond to user activity requires programming and is beyond the scope of our discussion. Instead, the discussion of how animation can be used will focus on the types of animations one can create using tools discussed in the previous section, without using associated scripting languages.

Animations have the ability to get attention, because we are drawn to movement. Advertisers have used this principle for many years, and their approach has varied over time. Advertisements started with crude animations, like flashing banner ads, and have evolved to sophisticated videos.

Animations have the capacity to entertain. Obvious examples of entertaining animations are cartoons like *The Simpsons, Looney Toons, South Park*, or the many Disney animated features. There are also notable examples of stop-motion animations, like *Wallace and Gromit*. Certain entertaining animations also carry a message and so are both entertaining and informative.

Animations can also be created to educate. For example, technical concepts, like how search engines work, can be animated. Figure 7.8 suggests a storyboard that might be used for this purpose. Such an animation could depict the programs that scour the internet for content as tiny robots. The robots could be shown reading the content on each web server and then updating the search engine. An animated version should be more visually engaging than a static version. Using a variety of techniques, like eye motion and eye contact, to enhance viewer engagement can lead to a high-impact educational experience.

FIGURE 7.8 A partial storyboard for an information animation

SUMMARY

Animation is a powerful means for gaining attention on the web. There is a wide range of animation software available, varying widely in cost and functionality. Despite widely different animating strategies embodied in various animation tools, most of these tools share common elements. The common functionality of animation tools revolves around the central objective of defining a sequence of frames. Therefore, all animation software must provide a means and an area for drawing and/or importing graphics to each frame. There must also be a mechanism for navigating from one frame to another, allowing the definition of a series of frames that will comprise an animation.

Animation tools vary in the relationship frames have to each other and how graphic elements are organized within a frame. The specific examples of animation software discussed in this chapter are Pencil, Adobe Flash, and Anime Studio. In Pencil, there is no relationship between frames, because one must create each frame from scratch. In stark contrast, in Studio and Adobe Flash, each frame shares the content from the preceding frames, unless the content is deleted or moved from the frame. Anime Studio will calculate a smooth transition for relocated, rotated, or resized elements if the animator specifies changes in graphic contents separated by one or more frames. Such a transition can also be created in Adobe Flash. Anime Studio and Adobe Flash allow graphic objects to be created out of a hierarchy of graphic components. That is, an animated character can contain other animated elements, like arms, legs, a mouth, and so on. Anime Studio creates such a hierarchy through a layer hierarchy, while Adobe Flash allows graphic objects to contain other graphic objects. Independent of what kind of animation software one uses, web-based animations can be used to entertain, inform and/or to gain attention.

CHAPTER EIGHT

CREATIVITY

POINTS TO CONSIDER

- Why is creative thought important for web development?
- What common misconceptions do people have concerning creative thinking?
- What is divergent creative thinking?
- What is convergent creative thinking?
- What sorts of challenges can one use convergent thinking for?
- Describe the creative thinking process attributed to Graham Wallas.
- Identify what one does at each stage of the above creative process.

- Give an example of using anthropomorphizing to create a new idea.
- Use role reversal to develop an original concept.
- How can exaggeration be used to comic effect?
- Give an example of using historically significant events to develop creative content.
- Synthesize two ideas to develop a new one. Do this repeatedly until an interesting idea emerges.

INTRODUCTION

Although this textbook focuses on technical and ethical aspects of web development, creative thought merits mention. The Web is full of opportunities for creativity. Web page content can be highly creative. Everything from narrative aspects of web page content to image compositions to animations and videos can benefit from creative ideas. By exploring creativity we have a greater opportunity to enhance web content and thereby garner a larger audience.

Conventional thinking about creative thought suggests that it is mysterious and impossible to characterize as a step-by-step process. Although one cannot reduce creative thinking into an algorithmic process, there are concrete techniques that one can employ to help with idea generation. This chapter will define a creative thinking process that will help demystify creative thinking and make it seem accessible to everyone. Before we embark on this endeavor, we will explore common misconceptions surrounding creative thought that inhibit people from more regularly engaging in creative thinking.

BARRIERS TO CREATIVE THINKING

All sorts of obstacles exist that discourage people from engaging in creative thought. They range from considering creative thinking a frivolous activity to assuming that we have no control over creative thought. We will try to dispel these myths and make a case that creative thought is a worthwhile endeavor.

Misconception: Creative Thought is a Frivolous Pursuit

Creative thinking involves developing original ideas. These ideas can be developed in response to a wide variety of needs and occur in many different domains. Some of these novel ideas may not be directed to solving a pressing need, while others may transform society in important ways. We can explore the breadth of areas that have benefited from revolutionizing creative ideas and the individuals who created them by reviewing Howard Gardner's investigation into the lives of Albert Einstein, T. S. Eliot, Sigmund Freud, Mahatma Gandhi, Martha Graham, Pablo Picasso, and Igor Stravinsky (Gardner, 1993). These individuals have changed society through their original contributions to the fields of physics, English, psychology, inter-personal thinking, kinesiology, spatial reasoning, and music respectively. Clearly, creative thinkers have transformed society in many important ways, dispelling the notion that creative thinking is a frivolous pursuit.

Misconception: Creative Thinking Requires Artistic Talent

Another common misconception is that one must have artistic talent in order to think creatively. The preceding section makes the case that creative thought is possible in all sorts of domains, many of which are not connected with art. Having artistic talent allows one an important outlet for certain creative ideas, however, many creative ideas can be established, even visually, without requiring artistic talent on the part of their generators. One illustration of this can be seen in a well-known animation called *Animator vs. Animation* by Alan Becker. In this animation, a stick figure, residing in an Adobe Flash development environment, develops its own behavior to combat the human who created it. The animation consists of basic line drawings and screen shots with edited elements copied from screen shots. No artistic talent is required to create this animation, and yet it exhibits a high level of originality.

There are many examples of highly creative visual expressions that require little or no artistic talent. Conceptual art such as Dadaist or Postmodernist art is rife with examples of highly touted works requiring no artistic talent, but much original thought. Marcel Duchamp's *L.H.O.O.Q.*, in which he takes a cheap reproduction of the Mona Lisa and adorns it with a mustache and goatee is such an example. Here he is expressing his ambivalence toward conventional art appreciation by showing disrespect toward a classic artwork, the *Mona Lisa*. Another example of conceptual art is Damien Hirst's work *The Physical Impossibility of Death in the Mind of Someone Living*, in which a thirteen-foot tiger shark is suspended in a tank of formaldehyde.

Generally speaking, many visual resources are available that do not require the creator to hand-render elements oneself. If one searches the Web for images, Google provides an advanced search option that allows specification of usage rights. This allows easy access to many visual artifacts. Also, most people have cell phones equipped with cameras, so digital photos can be easily taken. Thus, having artistic talent is not necessary to be creative.

Misconception: Creativity is Mysterious and We Have No Control Over It

When people think of a creative process, many think of a person sitting in a yoga position, patiently waiting for creative inspiration. Others assume that deep emotional experiences, such as sorrow or elation are necessary for creative inspiration. Others still believe that one is either innately capable of creativity or not. That is, that creative thinking is not something one can chose to engage in and actively pursue. This chapter will dispel these myths by presenting a pragmatic form of creative thinking and providing concrete techniques that will help assist in idea generation.

Although creativity is not completely understood, and there are less-well understood forms of creativity, there is much we do know. According to Michael LeBoeuf (1980), "The heart of all new ideas lies in the borrowing, adding, combining or modifying of old ones. Do it by accident and they'll call you lucky. Do it by design and they'll call you creative." This quote suggests a concrete process for idea generation. This chapter will lay out techniques that can help transform conventional ideas into creative ones.

Another useful quote concerning creativity is from Roger von Oech (1983). According to von Oech, "creative thinking involves imagining familiar things in a fresh light, digging below the surface to find previously undetected patterns, and finding connections among unrelated phenomena." This quote suggests that creativity involves a serious intellectual effort. This chapter will provide a set of intellectual exercises aimed at helping individuals transform more mundane ideas into novel ones.

In addition to various misconceptions about creative thought, there are other cultural barriers to engaging in creative idea exploration. Creativity often entails generating many possible ideas in a sort of trial-and-error manner. This means that many possible ideas must be rejected before more fruitful ideas can be pursued. In Western culture, failure must be avoided, so there is a barrier to engaging in this essential activity.

Many of the misconceptions concerning creativity result from people defining creativity as a divergent rather than a convergent thought process. The next section will look at these two forms of thought in more detail.

DIVERGENT AND CONVERGENT CREATIVE THINKING

When one feels that creative thinking is a mysterious process, one is thinking about divergent creative thought. Divergent thinking can lead to major paradigm-breaking ideas, or can come up empty. Examples of the results of divergent thought are the introduction of new forms of art, like abstract art, cubism, and impressionism. Divergent thought does not have a clear process that will lead to a solution. As a result, divergent thinking does not lend itself to established timeframes and deadlines. Divergent thinking is a high-risk, high-reward form of thought.

Convergent thinking is the more concrete, pragmatic form of creative thought, and will be addressed in this chapter. Convergent thinking, unlike divergent thought, can be characterized as a linear, step-by-step process, and as a result is more conducive to deadlines. Convergent thought is less risky than divergent thought, but generally results in less lofty ideas. In the context of this chapter we will discuss the development of creative visual elements for web pages, and so the creative goals will be clearly defined.

A Convergent Creative Process

Convergent thinking is better suited to solving creative challenges that have well-defined parameters, such as creating content for a website. Because a website addresses a well-defined content area, creative challenges in this context tend to be reasonably concrete. For example, the hiking website could benefit from having an animation on the hiking safety web page to emphasize certain safety principles. Having an animation could help communicate important information in an entertaining manner when that information might otherwise be ignored due to the perception that the content is dull.

A frequently cited process for creative idea development was introduced in 1926 by Graham Wallas (Lytton, 1971). Figure 8.1 identifies the four stages in Wallas' process which can be characterized as follows:

1. Preparation—In this stage the thinker seeks to expand or deepen his or her thinking about the subject matter at hand. This can take many forms, like brainstorming related concepts to develop a hierarchy of concepts. Another preparation activity is researching the topic in greater depth. For example, in the hiking website, one could embark on a hike with a heightened sense of awareness of the experience. One might make notes about one's feelings, the scenery, the flora and fauna, how the clothing looks or feels, or

Preparation
Incubation
Illumination
Verification

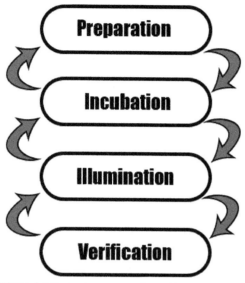

FIGURE 8.1 Typical convergent creative process

the equipment one uses during the hike. One may research stories about hikes, or visit a museum (in person or over the Internet) and view works of art that might provide inspiration either conceptually or stylistically. Other sources for inspiration could be literature, film, music, television, cartoons, or other websites.

It is important to record all the ideas and feelings that are generated during this phase, because they will be used in the next phase. The goal is to generate a large volume of ideas, feelings, and subject matter, so recording is necessary keep track of the volume of ideas. The more diversity of ideas that one generates, the more likely the next phase will be successful.

Figure 8.2 illustrates an initial phase of brainstorming for the hiking website. Two subject areas for the website are expanded, hiking and safety. The ideas laid out here are then further developed in the illustration.

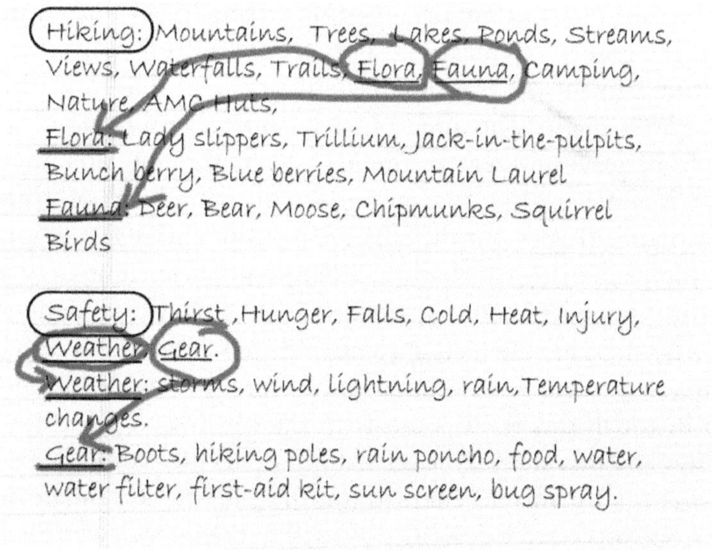

Hiking: Mountains, Trees, Lakes, Ponds, Streams,
Views, Waterfalls, Trails, Flora, Fauna, Camping,
Nature, AMC Huts,
Flora: Lady slippers, Trillium, Jack-in-the-pulpits,
Bunch berry, Blue berries, Mountain Laurel
Fauna: Deer, Bear, Moose, Chipmunks, Squirrel
Birds
Safety: Thirst, Hunger, Falls, Cold, Heat, Injury,
Weather, Gear.
Weather: storms, wind, lightning, rain, Temperature
changes.
Gear: Boots, hiking poles, rain poncho, food, water,
water filter, first-aid kit, sun screen, bug spray.

FIGURE 8.2 Initial brainstorming for the hiking website

2.   Incubation—In this phase one seeks to make the connections, combinations and transformations of the ideas generated in the previous phase to create innovative ideas. In this phase, it is important to distinguish a bizarre idea from a high-quality original idea. Although, one may develop a bizarre idea into an innovative idea with significant effort. A bizarre idea is one that falls flat when shown to a viewer of your website. In contrast, an innovative idea should have some impact on a viewer.

This phase of creative thinking is the most challenging for individuals who do not consider themselves creative or for those who have not engaged in creative thinking very frequently in the past. In order to help those who do not know where to start, a series of idea transformations will be presented here. Sample idea transformation techniques are the following:

a.   using anthropomorphism;
b.   using exaggeration;
c.   using role-reversal;
d.   jazzing up/ creating a visualization of a cliché;
e.   creating a visual metaphor;
f.   using historically significant events as inspiration;
g.   combing/synthesizing ideas;
h.   creating an analogy between two domains;
i.   using parody;
j.   looking at a concept extra-culturally; and
k.   Slap-stick.

Each transformation will be illustrated in the context of a Super Bowl advertisement in the next section. It is important to understand that during incubation, one should expect to generate many ideas before one finds a promising start to a creative concept.

3.   Illumination—In this phase, one recognizes the promise of a creative idea generated in the previous phase. The ability to recognize a promising idea is intellectually challenging. Experience in creative thinking helps develop this ability. It is important to note that idea generation does not end with the advent of a promising idea. During illumination one fleshes out the creative concept and makes it more concrete.

For example, during incubation, a marketing firm came up with the idea to anthropomorphize (apply human characteristics to) a stain on someone's shirt to illustrate the importance of having a stain removing stick. The initial concept was recognized as promising, so during illumination details were presumably filled in to flesh out a specific scenario in which this stain is most regrettable and to illustrate the point that if only that person had this stain remover with him, his life would be better.

The specifics for this ad entailed a rather dull-looking male at a job interview. The stain-bearing interviewee describes himself to the interviewer. Each time the interviewee speaks, the stain speaks in some gibberish. The interviewer is clearly captivated by the stain and cannot hear the interviewee over the stain. The stain becomes louder as the interviewee speaks, until it is yelling, to great comic effect. Throughout the interview, the interviewee has no idea that he is being overshadowed by the stain, adding to the humor of the situation. Another reason that this advertisement is highly entertaining is because the stain seems to have more personality than the interviewee, and the deadpan interviewer seems unable to give the interviewee any attention.

   This example illustrates that creative thinking continues throughout the illumination phase.

4. Verification—In this phase the concept is realized and tested using its target audience. As with the previous phase, creative thinking continues during this phase. For example, during the realization of the stain removal stick advertisement, additional decisions would be made in terms of what kind of voice the stain has, what hair cut the interviewee has, what kind of facial expressions the interviewer has in response to the stain's vocalizations, and so on.

At any point in the creative process, one may find that an idea is not working out as expected, and may need to return to a previous phase of the creative process. This return to a previous phase is suggested in figure 8.1 with the arrows pointing up to the previous phase.

   In order to better understand the techniques enumerated in the incubation phase for idea development, the next section identifies these techniques in Super Bowl ads.

ILLUSTRATING INCUBATION TECHNIQUES

According to superbowl-ads.com (2014), it costs an average of $4 million for a 30 second ad in 2014. As a result of the high expense of airing an ad, corporations invest a great deal of money in the creation of these ads, so one can expect the height of creativity to be embodied in these ads. These ads will be used to illustrate the incubation techniques enumerated in the previous section.

Using Anthropomorphism

Anthropomorphism is the application of human traits to inanimate objects or animals. In 2009, a traditional florist created an ad that attempted to distinguish florists that deliver a vase of flowers to customers from florists that deliver a box of flowers through postal services. The concept behind the ad was, "What does it say when you get a box of flowers instead of a vase of flowers?" The ad creators literally portrayed what the flowers would say by having them pop out of the box and speak to the recipient. As one might imagine, the flowers were not very nice, since the ad was intended to discourage boxed flowers. One flower starts with, "look at the mug on her face!" There arc a series of equally insulting outbursts from the flowers culminating in one flower exclaiming that no one would want to see the recipient naked.

The creative process continues after the decision to anthropomorphize the flowers to illustrate what boxed flowers say. The voice and the motion of the flowers, as well as the specific insults hurled by the flowers are important creative decisions. The context for the office delivery is also important to making the commercial entertaining.

Using Exaggeration

A well-executed example of an advertisement that uses exaggeration as its central creative device was introduced in 2009 by an on-line job site. The commercial starts with a view of the exterior of a handsome office building. The scene then rotates into the interior of an expansive manager's office, decorated in wood paneling with a mounted moose head on the wall. As the scene changes from the exterior of the building to the manager's office, the sound transitions from traffic noise to opera. The manager appears to be leisurely reading a newspaper with his feet on his neat desk. The scene continues to rotate through the walls into another office. The sound also transitions from opera to the sound of a dot-matrix printer. A prominent feature of this office is the body of the moose which is attached to the head in the manager's office. This office appears to be cramped with stacks of papers and boxes on an unattractive desk and filing cabinets. The worker in the office sits hunched over his desk under the back end of the moose. This exaggeration is taken to comedic effect. Laying out the specifics of each office and determining how the transition is made between offices demonstrate additional creative decisions beyond arriving at the initial creative concept.

Using Role Reversal

Role reversal entails exchanging the key characteristics of two characters. In 2012, a sports shoe manufacturer created commercial in which a short, squat French bulldog outruns a field of greyhounds. One would expect the French bulldog to be slow, but because it is wearing the right brand of sports shoe, it handily beats the greyhounds.

Jazzing Up/Creating a Visualization of a Cliché

In 2008, an online trading firm took the cliché, "it's so easy a baby could do it" and realized it visually by creating a hip, stock-trading baby. An online stock trading company would want to convince potential customers that using their software is easy, so this cliché is a natural choice. Transforming it to an entertaining commercial with a compelling message requires many creative decisions.

The baby takes on the voice of a hip twenty-something, as evidenced by the voice and choice of words, like "check it, you just saw me buy stock." The cliché is clearly in the ad creators' minds, as they have the baby say "if I (baby) can do it, you can do it." To remind the viewer how young the baby is, he spits up his milk, as very young babies are prone to do. The announcer at the end of the ad starts to recite the cliché, "it's so easy," but then ends with "there are a thousand new accounts a day."

Creating a Visual Metaphor

In 2010, a candy bar ad suggested we eat their candy bar to avoid hunger, because "you're not you, when you're hungry." The ad centers on a group of twenty-something men playing football. The only player not fitting the demographic is Betty White, who struggles to play, as an octogenarian. Upon getting a candy bar from a fan on the sideline, Betty White transforms into a fit young man, who then is able to play well, but is held back by his newly transformed teammate, Abe Vigoda. The specific choices made by the ad developers in terms of dialog and action made for a memorable and humorous ad. It was rated as one of the top three ads for the 2010 Super Bowl by the superbowl-ads.com website.

Using Historically Significant Events as Inspiration

The most notable ad that was inspired by a historical event is the 1983 Apple Corporation ad that was inspired by the George Orwell book, 1984. The ad announced the introduction of its new line of computers to be available in 1984. It is considered to be one of the all-time great ads by the superbowl-ads.com website. In 1983, Apple Corporation was trying to distinguish itself from its primary competitor, IBM. In the ad Apple represents itself as a kind of David and Goliath character, where Apple is David and IBM is the Orwellian Big Brother/Goliath. The David character is a woman in a vibrantly colored running outfit carrying a sledgehammer. She runs into an auditorium populated with monochrome, drone-like people watching a projection of an equally monochrome Big Brother figure making Orwellian pronouncements. The David-figure hurls her sledgehammer into the projection screen, causing it to explode. The commercial concludes with an announcer proclaiming that Apple's new product will prevent 1984 from becoming "1984." In addition to the inspiration of historical events, using the David and Goliath story creates a masterful ad, appealing to our instinct to support the underdog.

Other examples of Super Bowl ads that use historical events include a car manufacturer using the Mayan prediction that the world will end in 2012 and the twenty-fifth anniversary of Michael Jackson's *Thriller* album. The Mayan apocalypse ad features an urban landscape full of smoldering ash and rubble. One sees a torn newspaper blowing in the wind with a headline referring to the Mayan prediction. One hears the start of an engine and then a truck emerges from a pile of rubble. A small group of men gather in a clearing, all with trucks from the advertiser's brand. One of the men asks the others where Dave is. One of the men responds that Dave drove a truck from the leading competitor. The commercial ends when it starts to rain frogs.

Combing/Synthesizing Ideas

Most creative ideas are the result of combining or/and or synthesizing two or more ideas. The Apple ad outlined in the previous section synthesized the ideas from the novel *1984* and the story of David and Goliath to create one of the all-time great ads. On occasion, the ideas being synthesized are a bit bizarre, so getting them to work effectively requires additional creativity.

In 2008, a beer company combined light beer and fire breathing in their ad. The idea behind the ad is that drinking light beer by this manufacturer will give the drinker super powers, like the ability to breathe fire. The ad involves a male suitor having dinner at the home of a woman. He takes a sip of beer and wishes to impress the woman with his ability to breathe fire by lighting the candles with his breath. He then begins to sneeze, which also causes him to throw flames. He asks if his dinner host has a cat. The ad ends with a view of a charred woman and her cat.

This combination of ideas was relatively risky, but the beer company succeeded in creating an entertaining narrative.

Creating an Analogy Between Two Domains

In 2008, a women's lingerie retailer created an ad predicated on the connection between the game of football and the game of love. The ad featured a seductive model clad in lingerie playfully handling a football. Interspersed with shots of the model is text that reminded the viewers that the football game was almost over and that the *real* game would soon begin. The analogy itself was reasonably clever, but it was executed in a relatively uninteresting manner.

Parody

In 2010, a light beer company created an ad spoofing the popular television series *Lost*. In the ad the passengers are dusting themselves off after the crash of the plane, when one of the passengers finds that the radio equipment is still functional, and they may be able to leave the island as a result. The other passengers seem uninterested in this discovery. A moment later another passenger discovers an intact beverage cart, full of a particular brand of light beer. The passengers react enthusiastically to this, and a party breaks out. One passenger exclaims that everything is going to be all right as a result of the light beer. An additional humorous element is introduced as the woman who discovers the radio equipment finds a signal, but another passenger changes the controls to play dance music, and the party continues.

Look at a Concept Extra-Culturally

This technique is particularly challenging, because individuals tend to be so immersed in their respective cultures that it is difficult to determine how to step outside of it. In 2009, a free television streaming website gave a startlingly candid assessment of the quality of much of what is televised. Under the guise of a space alien's perspective, TV content was characterized as mind melting. Using a well-known actor to portray the alien provided the initial appeal of the ad. The final image one is left with is that of an alien drooling at the prospect of eating a human brain, after the mindless content of television has reduced that brain to mush.

Slapstick

Generally not considered to be the height of creativity, slapstick is an easy fallback, when all else fails. One may also add an element of slapstick to punctuate another creative concept, as an add-on. In 2011, an updated version of the candy bar ad that was discussed under the "creating visual metaphor" category used the same metaphor, "you're not you when you're hungry." They used a different context. This time rather than football the metaphor is visualized in a lumber yard. At the end of the commercial a lumber yard worker who was transformed into Rosanne Bar is hit and knocked down by a swinging log, providing a bit of slapstick humor.

Although slapstick often does not result in an intellectually laudable idea, it can be a good starting point if one is having trouble developing an original idea.

Applying the Incubation Phase to the Hiking Website

A very fruitful idea transformation technique for creating animations is anthropomorphism. A relatively easy way to start the incubation phase in the hiking website is to take the results of a second-level brainstorming process, as shown in Figure 8.3, and try applying certain incubation techniques to it, like anthropomorphism. Figure 8.4 shows possible candidates for applying this transformation technique. The candidates are all non-human objects or animals that one can imagine as making an interesting animation. Sometimes, one may need to generate additional ideas for the brainstorming phase, so that suitable ideas are available for anthropomorphizing. For example, in the salty snack category, animating a bag of potato chips seems better than animating a pickle, because people are more apt to bring a bag of chips on a hike than a pickle. Another example of idea substitution is apparent when contemplating anthropomorphizing a bug. One needs to consider the specific type of bug one is likely to encounter. The animation of a tick would differ greatly from a black fly or mosquito, for example.

Possible anthropomorphisms from the objects generated by Figure 8.4 are as follows:

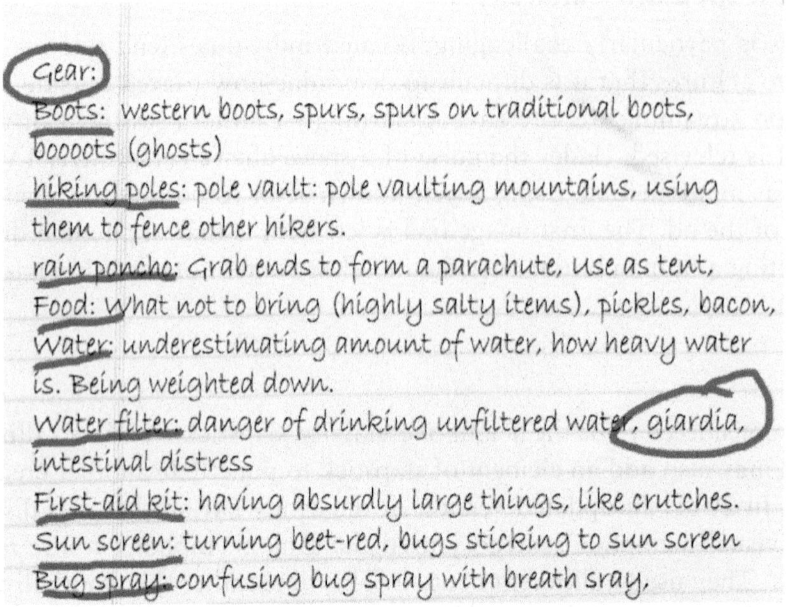

Gear:
Boots: western boots, spurs, spurs on traditional boots, booooots (ghosts)
hiking poles: pole vault: pole vaulting mountains, using them to fence other hikers.
rain poncho: Grab ends to form a parachute, use as tent,
Food: What not to bring (highly salty items), pickles, bacon,
Water: underestimating amount of water, how heavy water is. Being weighted down.
Water filter: danger of drinking unfiltered water, giardia, intestinal distress
First-aid kit: having absurdly large things, like crutches.
Sun screen: turning beet-red, bugs sticking to sun screen
Bug spray: confusing bug spray with breath sray,

FIGURE 8.3 A second phase of brainstorming

Candidates for anthropomorphizing
Gear:
Boots: booooots (ghosts)
hiking poles: pole vault: pole vaulting mountains, using them to fence other hikers.
rain poncho: Grab ends to form a parachute, use as tent,
Replace with potato chip
Food: What not to bring (highly salty items), pickles, bacon,
Water: underestimating amount of water, how heavy water is. Being weighted down.
Water filter: danger of drinking unfiltered water, giardia, intestinal distress
First-aid kit: having absurdly large things, like crutches.
Sun screen: turning beet-red, bugs sticking to sun screen
Bug spray: confusing bug spray with breath sray,
ticks
mosquitos
black flies

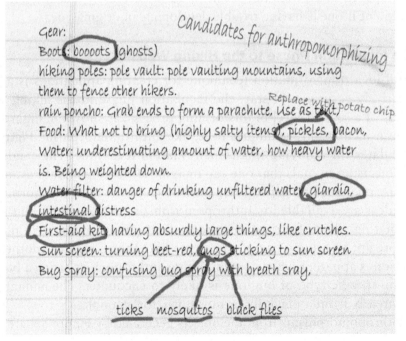

FIGURE 8.4 Anthropomorphizing ideas

1. Haunted boooots. Spirits from past hikers inhabiting the boot warn the hiker of various perils that one may encounter along the trail.
2. The hiker eats a bag of potato chips, but then the chips continually remind the hiker how thirsty he/she is.
3. A hiker drinks from a clear stream and gets infected with the giardia bacteria. The bacteria are shown as crazy and annoying companions that the hiker can never get rid of.
4. After drinking water from a stream the intestines become vocal and remind the hiker of their presence.
5. A tick carrying Lyme disease jumps off a bush and onto a hiker. The tick then finds a remote spot on the hiker to set up its camp and raise its family.
6. Mosquitos and/or black flies are portrayed as dive-bombing squadrons.

Incubation techniques provide procedures for idea generation. This allows individuals who are new to creative thinking a means to make progress. Of course, not all ideas generated by incubation techniques are of good quality. The ability to recognize an idea that has potential requires some insight and practice to do effectively. This is the goal of the next phase of the creative process, illumination. The illumination phase is necessary to determine which, if any, of the previous anthropomorphisms might make a fruitful animation.

ILLUMINATION

The previous phases of the creative process provide a means to generate a volume of ideas. Most of these ideas will not be high-quality creative ideas and should be rejected. Illumination occurs when an idea is recognized as showing great promise. There is no procedure for making such a determination. This phase requires intellectual effort to correctly reject bad ideas and to see the potential in good ones.

Additional intellectual and creative ability is required to transform the kernel of an idea into a fully fleshed out concept. So, creative decisions are often made during the illumination phase. For example, in the online investing ad where the core concept was "it's so easy a baby could do it," many creative decisions were required to transform the central idea into the baby with the voice, dialog, and context of the specific ad. Many other ads for this investment firm have been developed around this core idea since 2008, illustrating the versatility of the core idea. These spin-off ads take the same central concept and vary the dialog and context.

Creativity researchers have determined several personality traits that are associated with successful creative thinking. These characteristics are particularly important for the illumination phase. These characteristics are (Hennessey, 2010) (Feist, 2010):

1. willingness to overcome obstacles;
2. willingness to take sensible risks;
3. self-efficacy; and
4. motivation.

The above personality traits suggest a person who has enough motivation to discard many bad or merely adequate ideas in order to find a high-quality idea has the requisite traits to be creative. It also suggests someone who has good judgment to weed out the bad ideas and to recognize and develop more promising ideas.

The illumination process can be characterized as a form of cost-benefit analysis. One needs to perceive a clear benefit from creating the work in question. The benefit can be that the work is educational, entertaining, persuasive, inspirational or beautiful, or some combination of these objectives. After the benefit has been identified then the effort required needs to be contemplated. Because the work is still very early in its development, the estimates of effort required to complete the work is understood to be preliminary.

In order to illustrate the illumination process, the ideas generated during the incubation phase will be evaluated. It should be noted again that the brainstorming and incubation phases have been abbreviated in this chapter to conserve space. Brainstorming would normally continue by expanding upon more categories of ideas. Similarly, the incubation phase would normally explore more than one idea transformation technique.

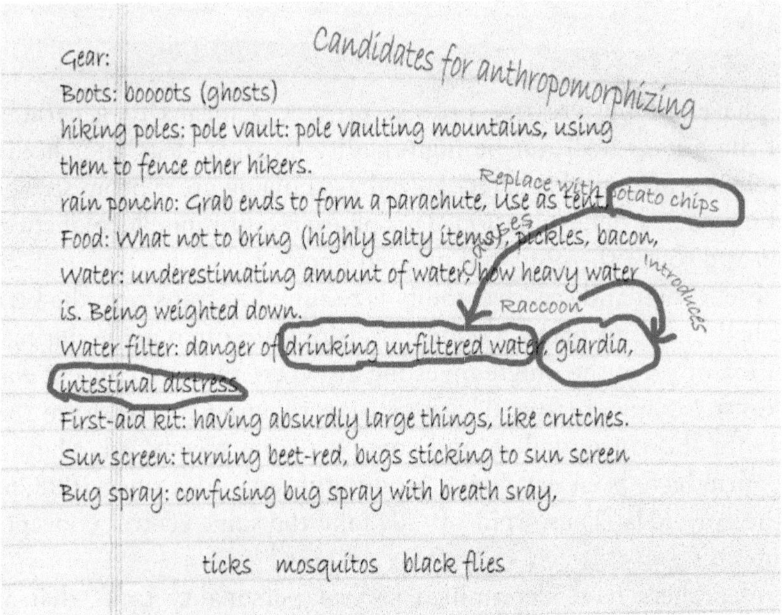

FIGURE 8.5 Starting the illumination phase

The Illumination Phase and the Hiking Website

The illumination phase begins by considering the results of the previous phase of the creative thought process. Normally, one would proceed having attempted more than a single idea- transformation technique during incubation, but in the spirit of brevity, we will evaluate the abbreviated results to illustrate this phase.

In the previous phase of creative thinking section, six possibilities were generated. The first idea resulted from playing with the word boots and transforming it into boooots, as in the "boo" one exclaims in order to frighten someone. The term also conjures up the specter of ghosts. The central idea is to have the boots speak to the hiker, explaining the history of fatal accidents that have occurred along the trail as those locations are encountered during the hike. The boots would conjure up the ghost of each victim. The result could be a dramatic and very useful animation, and thus a successful creative work. The project could be an entertaining way to disseminate some sobering information about the dangers of hiking certain trails. However, there is a high-risk element to this project. Acquiring the information about these fatalities could be difficult. This project merits further research to determine if this information is easily accessible. If not, the effort to investigate these fatalities could make the project prohibitively time consuming. This idea should be identified as meriting further consideration, but other ideas should be evaluated in the interim.

The next idea involves animating a salty snack to pester the hiker about his/her need to hydrate. The story would entail the hiker exhausting his/her supply of water as a result of having eaten the bag of potato chips with, hopefully, amusing reminders by the snack as to the constant thirst. Although this idea seems as though it could be more profound, the amount of effort required to implement the animated snack versus the anticipated reward of creating an entertaining and informative animation is not high enough to pursue this option. The other ideas merit further evaluation.

FIGURE 8.6 Possible characters from left to right: Giardia, raccoon, and pirate tick

The third idea entails reminding hikers that, although New Hampshire's clear streams and rivers look inviting, one should not drink from them, due to the parasites that one might ingest. While envisioning the story that will be used to make this point, a specific parasite, giardia, is researched to help with imagining the details. By looking at photographs of the parasite, it is easier to imagine a cartoon version. The animation will make an impact by emphasizing the possibility that a giardia infection may not be simply an unpleasant and painful experience during the hike, but may be a long-term companion years after the hike. The parasite is envisioned to be an entertaining character, so the entertainment/education benefit is projected to be high. The implementation is non-trivial, but not excessively difficult. This idea seems to have promise, but isn't so appealing that idea evaluation should cease.

The fourth idea is similar to the last one in that the goal is also to discourage drinking unfiltered water from natural water sources. In this case, the anthropomorphism centers on the complaining intestines. This concept varies the focus from the parasite to the result of the infection. This animation addresses the short-term consequences, rather than the possibility of long-term infection by the parasite. This idea seems less appealing than the giardia idea, so further exploration is appropriate.

The fifth idea is unrelated to drinking water. It is about the danger of ticks. The greatest danger of ticks is the possibility of acquiring Lyme disease. By playing with the term Lyme

FIGURE 8.7 Story board for the hiking website

and transforming it into *limey*, the term used to refer to pirates due to their tendency to have scurvy, a pirate-like tick is easy to imagine. The tick could swing on a rope from a plant unto the unwitting person, making itself comfortable and getting drunk on the hiker's blood. There is clear potential is this concept, because there is value in educating hikers about Lyme disease and the tick could be an entertaining character. The animation is anticipated to be moderately challenging, so there is potential in this concept.

The final idea reminds hikers that mosquitos and black flies can make hiking without bug repellent unpleasant. This idea seems somewhat less educationally relevant than the previous idea. Also, the particulars of the concept, namely the dive-bombing idea, seem too similar to bug spray ads that have already been made, so the analysis results in idea rejection.

So far the analysis has netted four ideas that have enough potential to move forward, however there is none that is a decisive winner. So, at this point we may elect to return to the incubation phase and generate more ideas, or try to further develop the ideas at hand until one seems strong enough to pursue. In reviewing the ideas for further development, three ideas are noted as being sequentially connected. The ideas relating to the drinking water could be sequenced as the salty snack causes thirst, followed by the hiker ingesting giardia, causing the intestines to become vocal. This creates a more interesting story, but also a longer animation. So, as the benefit increases, so does the cost of implementing it.

In the final analysis the giardia, is anticipated to be an entertaining story-line, so the educational animation will start with this concept and expand on the idea by creating a cute raccoon to serve as the source of the giardia. If the time commitment is not prohibitive, other related ideas can be added. The success of this creative idea rests on how well the idea is fleshed out. The details will be determined during implementation, which occurs during the verification phase.

VERIFICATION

During the illumination phase, a series of ideas from the incubation phase is evaluated. The illumination phase results in a candidate idea for development. The goal of the verification phase is to continue to flesh out the creative details and to bring the concept into existence. There are many more creative decisions that must be made during verification before the concept is made real. There is no step-by-step procedure that can assist during this phase. The quality of the outcome depends on the skill, motivation, and experience of the creator.

The real goal of verification is to confirm the quality of the concept. The first step in verifying this concept is to make the idea real and to evaluate it as the creator. After you have made any adjustments, the next step in verification is to get audience reaction to the work. Finding members of the target audience and getting their honest reaction is the ultimate verification for a creative work. As the creator, you want to ask yourself if the work accomplishes the goals that that you initially set out for it. You should then assess the audience feedback in this context.

Examples of creative decisions that can be made during verification:

1. specifying look of characters;
2. determining dialogue, if relevant;
3. selecting voice of characters, if relevant;
4. selecting specific actions; and
5. determining the look of the background and props in a scene.

To provide a more concrete illustration of the verification phase, the hiking website safety animation will be discussed.

The Verification Phase and the Hiking Website

In order to complete planning for the hiking website animation, the storyline for the animation should be made more specific using a storyboard. Figure 8.7 illustrates a possible storyboard characterizing each scene. Recall that the goal of the animation is to discourage hikers from drinking unfiltered water due to the possibility of getting a persistent infection by the giardia parasite. The storyboard should be read from top to bottom and from left to right. Each scene can be described as follows:

1. The source for the giardia is shown as a raccoon taking a drink from the stream and then defecating.
2. The giardia is shown as growing and reproducing.
3. The hiker is shown hiking over a mountain and then taking a drink from the stream.
4. The final scene shows the giardia hitching along with the hiker, being annoying.

An additional creative choice that needs to be made in order to complete the animation is how to communicate the onerousness of the giardia for the hiker. So, there is one last big creative decision to be made.

After the animation is completed, the animator should critique the animation and make any necessary adjustments. Finally, the animation should be shown to its target audience members to determine its ultimate success.

SUMMARY

With the volume of web content available, creative content is a means to distinguish oneself and attract an audience. Although many consider creative thought beyond their capability, we are all capable of engaging in creative thinking. The form of creative thinking addressed in this chapter is known as convergent thinking, and is best suited to taking on concrete challenges. The specific creative process outlined here was created by Graham Wallas, and consists of four stages, preparation, incubation, illumination, and verification. Specific activities and techniques were outlined by which one may engage in the preparation and incubation phases, where one generates and transforms ideas respectively. The illumination and verification phases require more experience in creative thinking to do well, and it is difficult to provide concrete means to go about these phases. The illumination phase can entail a form of cost-benefit analysis as one evaluates ideas generated by the incubation phase for further consideration. Creative idea generation continues throughout the entire process, including the verification phase, where one realizes the creative concept.

REFERENCES

Feist, G. J. (2010). The function of personality in creativity: The nature and nurture of the creative person. In J. C. Kaufman, J.C. and Sternberg R. J. *The Cambridge handbook of creativity*. (pp. 113–130). New York, NY, U.S.: Cambridge University Press.

Gardner, H. (1993). *Creating minds: An anatomy of creativity seen through the lives of Freud, Einstein, Picasso, Stravinsky, Eliot, Graham, and Gandhi*. New York, NY U.S.: Basic Books.

Hennessey, B. A. (2010). The creativity–motivation connection. In J.C. Kaufman & R. J. Sternberg (Eds.), *Cambridge handbook of creativity* (pp. 342–365). New York, NY: Cambridge University Press.

LeBoeuf, M. (1980). *Imagineering*. New York: McGraw-Hill.

Lytton, H. (1971) *Creativity and Education*. London: Routledge & Kegan Paul, pp. 10–18.

Superbowl-ads.com. (2014). Super Bowl Broadcast News. Retrieved June 30, 2014 from http://superbowl-ads.com/article_archive/.

Von Oech, R. (1983). *A Whack on the Side of the Head: how to unlock your mind for innovation*. New York: Warner Books, Inc.

CHAPTER NINE

USING SOUND ON THE WEB

POINTS TO CONSIDER

- What is sound?
- How is sound digitized?
- What options are there for digitizing sounds?
- What trade-offs are there when minimizing sound file size?
- What types of sound files are there, and what are their properties?
- What file type would you select for a long narrative and why?
- Why are MIDI files less common on the web?

- List five major categories of functionality that *Audacity* is capable of.
- Name five different ways to use sound on a website.
- Why is sound difficult to use well on the web?
- Name as many effective uses of sound on the web as possible.
- Name three poor uses of sound on the web.

INTRODUCTION

Sound is one of the most challenging media types to use effectively on the web. When done well, sound can enhance someone's experience at a website. When sound is used poorly, it can lengthen web page download times and annoy or repel people. Another complexity regarding the use of sound on the Internet is that music is heavily copyrighted. So, if you purchase a song, you own the music file or CD, but not rights to distribute it over the Internet. One of the more positive aspects of using sound on the Internet is that there is wonderful software available at no cost for recording and editing your own narration, sounds, or music.

This chapter will begin by exploring the basic principles of sound. We will then look at how sound is digitally recorded and discuss different sound file formats. Next, the sound editing software, Audacity, will be explored, and some design suggestions will be made for effective use of sound on websites. Finally, some brief how-to information will be provided for including sound on a web page.

WHAT IS SOUND?

In order to understand sound, one can think about a typical source of sound, a drum. Figure 9.1 shows a drum stick that is about to strike the surface of a drum. When the impact occurs, the drum's membrane vibrates. This vibration is transmitted to the air, which propagates the vibration to our ears. Depending on one's perspective, sound is either the vibration that is propagated through the air, or the vibration that is perceived as a result of the vibration on our eardrums.

The air vibration associated with a sound is known as a *sound wave*, and is often represented as a sine wave, as shown in Figure 9.2. Each sound has a set of properties that can be

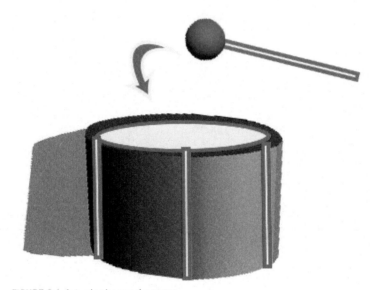

FIGURE 9.1 A typical sound source

represented on a sine wave. Each sound has the characteristics of pitch, volume, and duration. Figure 9.2 expresses these properties in terms of a sine wave as frequency, amplitude, and time, respectively. Frequency influences the pitch of a sound. Frequency is the width of the sine wave. This measurement extends from the beginning of a wave until the same position in the next wave. A wide frequency relates to a lower pitch than a narrow wave. The amplitude of the wave measures the height of the sine wave from top to bottom of the wave and relates to the loudness of a sound. The higher the amplitude, the louder the sound is. Finally, the longer the sound waves persist on the timeline the longer the sound is.

Having a rudimentary understanding of sound is helpful for understanding how sound is digitized. The next section will use the sine wave representation to explain how sound waves are digitized.

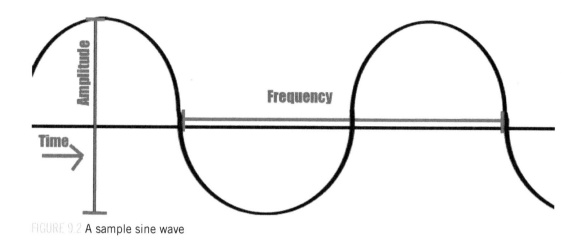

FIGURE 9.2 A sample sine wave

HOW SOUND IS DIGITIZED

In order to use sound on a website, it must be converted into a form that can be stored in a computer file. So, sound must be converted from its continuous, analog sine wave form into discrete sample points that can then be stored in a computer file. Figure 9.3 shows a hypothetical sampling of a sound wave. The red dots in the figure represent sample points in the wave. When taking samples, there are two basic choices that one can make. The first choice is how often to take samples. The more samples one takes, the closer the digitized sound will resemble the original and the larger the sound file will be. Since these files will be transmitted over the Internet, the smaller the better, but not so small that the perceived sound quality deteriorates. Ideally, the digitized file should have sufficient samples to reproduce the sound with reasonable quality, while not being so large that it causes delays in downloading a web page. Because the highest frequency humans can hear is 20,000 Hz (Burnie 1995), a sampling rate at twice this rate is sufficient to capture all sounds that are perceptible to the human ear. A music CD records music at 44,100 Hz, for example (Self 2009).

Another choice to be made when digitizing sound is how many bits to use to express the amplitude of each sample. The more bits one uses, the more precisely one can express the amplitude of the sound wave. This means that the loudness or softness of a sound can be more accurately represented. The size of the sound file is influenced by the number of bits used per sample. An audio CD typically uses a sample size of 16 bits (Self 2009). The sound editing tool to be discussed in this chapter, Audacity, supports 16-, 24-, and 32-bit sample sizes.

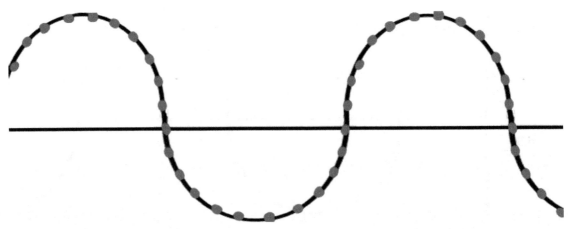

FIGURE 9.3 Sampling a sound wave

How Sound is Digitally Recorded and Played

In order to record sound one needs a microphone to pick up the sound vibrations. The microphone transmits this analog signal to an analog-to-digital converter (ADC), which is found on a computer's sound card. The ADC samples the analog signal at the specified sample rate (44,100 Hz, for example) by recording the amplitude of the sound. This information is stored in a file.

Playing a sound file takes the digital information stored in the sound file and converts it into an analog signal using a digital-to-analog converter (DAC), which is found on a sound card. The analog signal is then amplified and played using the computer's speakers.

The entire recording and playback process is summarized in Figure 9.4. The figure shows a microphone picking up the sound and transmitting the signal to the analog-to-digital converter on the sound card. The sound file is saved on a storage device like the computer's hard drive. When the sound is played, it is retrieved from the storage device and converted back to an analog signal and sent to the computer's speakers.

There is another piece of information pertaining to the digitizing of sound that merits discussion, namely sound file formats. Some common options in sound file types will be explored next.

SOUND FILE FORMATS

The topic of sound file formats refers to the manner in which the sound information is organized in the sound file. There are a number of options. One can classify the file formats

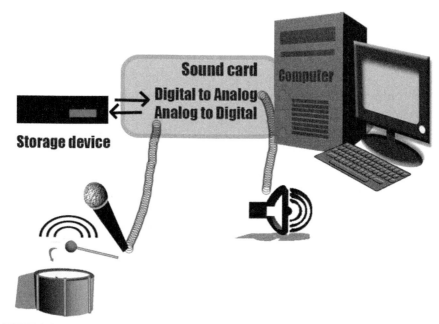

FIGURE 9.4 The digital recording and playback process

into four basic categories: compressed, pulse code modulated (PCM), streaming, and Musical Instrument Digital Interface (MIDI).

Streaming audio files are files in which audio information is progressively sent to the receiving computer while it is being played. Non-streaming audio files must be completely downloaded before they can be played. Streaming audio files requires special support from the web server, and is beyond the scope of this text.

The most common non-streaming audio file formats on the web are categorized as either *PCM* or *compressed*. The final category of sound file, MIDI, is less common, but may become more popular in the future. PCM files are sampled in the manner described in the previous section without compression, whereas compressed audio files are initially sampled like the PCM files, but are then reduced in size using a compression strategy. Examples of PCM file formats are Waveform Audio File format (WAV) and Sun Microsystems' Simple Audio format (AU) files. Examples of compressed audio files are MPEG-1 or MPEG-2 Audio Layer III (MP3) and Ogg Vorbis, a nonproprietary container format.

Web browsers generally need additional software enhancements, known as plug-ins, to play each type of music file. So, WAV files require one plug-in and MP3 files require another. Adding plug-in software is generally easy to do.

Some common web-based audio file formats follow.

- WAV—Created for computers running the MS Windows operating system. Because it is an uncompressed (PCM) sound format, it is best suited to short sounds, like sound effects.
- AU—is an older format. It is generally PCM or uncompressed, and is not as common as the .wav format.
- MP3—this is a compressed format, and is currently the most popular music file format.
- Ogg—is an open-source format that encapsulates multiple music formats. It is not as popular as MP3, however.
- WMA—Windows Media Audio is an MS Windows format that supports copyright protection.
- RA (Real Audio) and RM (Real Media)—are used for streaming audio content over the Internet.

MIDI Audio Files

One could consider the MIDI sound format to be the vector file analog of audio content. As you recall from the section on representing image files, vector images are a concise representation of images, because they express images through higher-level geographic shapes rather than individual pixels. In a similar manner, MIDI files express higher-level notes from specific instruments, as opposed to a sampling from a sound signal. Like vector files, MIDI files are extremely small in comparison to the equivalent PCM or compressed audio files, so their size would make them ideal for web development. However, there is a drawback to MIDI files, because they require a substantial software infrastructure. Web browsers do not generally embed this support, so MIDI files are not commonly found on web pages. This lack of web browser support may change in the future.

Now that we have a sense of how digital sound works and the file format options available, we can discuss how to create digital sound files. We will look at a sound editing/recording program, called Audacity, that is freely available on the Internet.

AUDACITY

Audacity is a powerful, yet easy-to-use, sound recording/editing application developed by two individuals from Carnegie Mellon University. It is open-source and freely available over the Internet, and is available at software distribution sites, like sourceforge.net. It can also be used to convert sound file formats. For example, one could take a WAV file and compress it into an MP3 format file to create a compressed file. Figure 9.5 shows its interface. The main controls for Audacity handle the primary functions of an audio recorder,

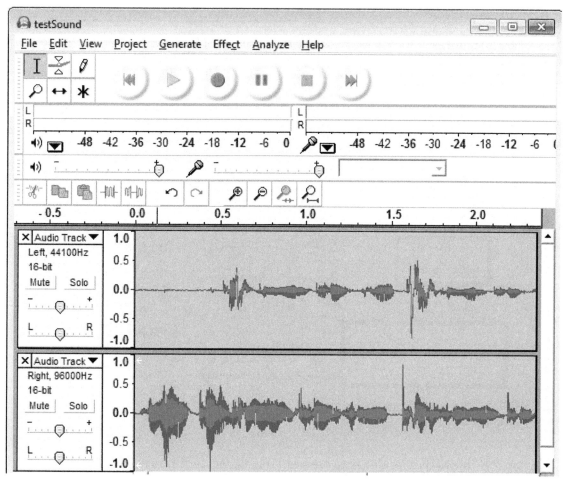

FIGURE 9.5 Sample Audacity Interface
Source: Audacity / (CC BY 3.0).

like play, record, stop, and pause. These are shown as buttons, much like a conventional audio recorder.

In addition to basic recording and playback features, Audacity supports sound editing capabilities. One can copy tracks by selecting certain tracks and selecting the copy option under the edit menu, or by using the CTRL+C key shortcut, as one might do using a word processor. One may also integrate multiple tracks together. It is also possible to assign tracks to either the left or right channel in a stereo sound file. Figure 9.5 shows two tracks that will be combined to create the sound file. One may also apply a variety of effects to portions of a sound track by selecting a desired section of a sound track. For example, one can apply a pitch change to raise the pitch of narration to create a comical effect.

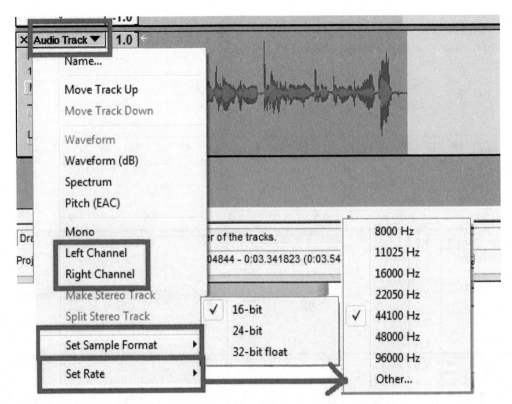

FIGURE 9.6 Audacity audio track pull-down box options
Source: Audacity / (CC BY 3.0).

Figure 9.6 shows the options that are available in the audio track pull-down box. Red rectangles have been added to the interface to draw the reader's attention to particular areas of the software's interface. Each track may be assigned to either left/right/or neither (mono). Also, specifications for sampling can be assigned to each tracking. Options for the sampling rate and sampling format are shown in Figure 9.6. The example shows that 44,100 Hz has been selected as the sample rate and the sample format is 16-bit.

Audacity has many more features than what has been outlined in this section, but the previously discussed capabilities are a good starting point for audio development. The area of sound effects is worth additional mention. A few of Audacity's sound effects are listed below.

- Amplify
- Change pitch
- Change speed
- Echo
- Equalization

- Fade in/fade out
- Noise removal

In addition to creating your own sounds, various sound files are available on the Internet. Free sound effects can be downloaded from a number of websites. Music files are harder to come by, but sites like opsound.org and Wikimedia.org have music files that are free to use.

Integrating sound effectively into website content is extremely challenging from a design perspective. Although sound can readily attract attention, it can also be annoying or repellent. The next section addresses some basic design considerations for using sound on a website.

DESIGN CONSIDERATIONS

It is extremely challenging to use sound well on a website, so careful consideration should be given before integrating sound into one's site. Also, good use of sound can vary widely depending on one's audience. For example, using sound effectively on a children's website is radically different from a website geared to an adult audience. There are a number of ways that one can use sound on a website. The following are some examples.

- Background music
- Narration
- Sound effects
- Music/narration in an animation
- Music/narration in a video
- Alert for an error
- Alert for drawing attention (e.g., advertisement)

Most of these uses for sound are unadvisable. Unless the website is about music or for children, background music is not a good idea for a number of reasons. Not all of the website's audience may enjoy the selected music. The music may slow the loading of the web page excessively. Finally, the music may interfere with adaptive devices, like screen readers, for people with visual or reading disabilities. If narration is an option that accompanies a text-based option, this could be a good use of sound. Complexities of using sound in animation or videos include the previous concerns and have the added issues of being annoying due to the possibility of the animation or video looping.

Internet-based games are also a good use of sound. Games often contain background music and sound effects. Certain games also contain narration.

A good use of sound involves using sound to alert people of certain special situations. Of course, as a website designer, one cannot rely on audio prompts as the only means to alert individuals, because some people will have their sound muted or turned down. Responding to people's data entry and clicks, beyond the use of hyperlinks, is beyond the scope of this text, however.

Audio should be used with great care on a website. The next challenge is to determine how one can include sound on a website. The next section briefly touches on how-to information regarding the use of sound.

HOW TO ADD SOUND TO A WEBSITE

Using sound in animations and video is generally supported by most animation and video tools. Some tools include sound recording capabilities. Other tools allow the importing of sound files. As previously mentioned, using sound in response to data entry or mouse clicks is beyond the scope of this text, so we will briefly illustrate another use of sound on a web page. In this example, a heavily narrative page provides an option to play an audio version of the text. Figure 9.7 illustrates what such a page could look like. It is important to note that the audio player is not set to automatically start playing, so the audio is strictly optional.

How sound is added to a web page has changed significantly with the introduction of the new HTML5 standard. Sound file formats currently supported by the new standard are MP3, WAV, and Ogg. Embedding sound using Amaya is not currently supported through the graphical user interface (GUI), while it is supported using Adobe Dreamweaver's GUI. However, one can still add sound using Amaya by going into *view source* mode and adding the HTML instructions directly.

To add sound using Adobe Dreamweaver, open the desired web page and place the cursor where the sound player should appear. Next, select the menu option *Insert → Media →HTML5 Audio*. Figure 9.8 shows the window that appears in response to the menu selections. In this window specify the sound file in the *Source* field. You may also provide a title to the audio and specify *fallback text,* which is text that appears if a browser does not support playing this sound file. There are also two possible alternate sound files that can be specified, should the first sound file not play. The alternate sound files can be specified in the *Alt Source 1* and *Alt Source 2* fields, so that if the web browser does not support the first type of sound file, it can try other options, if specified. Finally, the *Autoplay* checkbox should remain unchecked, so that the sound can be manually started.

To add sound to a web page using Amaya currently requires the addition of HTML instructions. This means that the HTML must be viewed by selecting *Show source* under

FIGURE 9.7 Using sound on a website

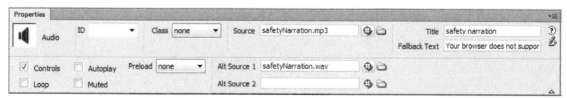

FIGURE 9.8 Window used to add sound files using Adobe Dreamweaver
Source: Adobe Systems Incorporated.

the *View* menu options. The HTML equivalent for adding the sound file in the previous section is shown below.

```
<audio title="safety narration" controls >
<source src="safetyNarration.MP3" type="audio/MP3" />
<source src="safetyNarration.wav" type="audio/wav" />
<p>Your browser does not support playing this sound file</p>
</audio>
```

The above HTML starts with the audio tag that includes an optional title. The title appears when the cursor hovers over the audio player. It is important to include controls for the audio, since sound should generally be optional, and this allows the elective playing of the sound file. Using the word *controls* causes controls to appear, while omitting the word causes the controls to be absent. The URL for the sound file is specified in the *sound* tag. Multiple sound files are specified in case a web browser cannot play the first option. The final element of the audio component is text surrounded by the <p> and </p> tag pair. This is the *fallback* text message that appears in the event that the web browser is unable to play any of the sound files.

When adding HTML directly to the source code, it is important to ensure that the placement of the instructions does not disrupt existing HTML instructions. One should place the cursor in a position that is not inside another start/end tag pair. For example, the following instruction shows a link.

```
<a href="safetyInfo2.html">click for more safety information ... </a>
```

The begin and end tags for the link are <a> and </a>, and nothing should be added between them. On the other hand, the audio *must* be between the begin and end tags for the *body* of the HTML document, which looks like this: <body> and </body>. Other tag pairs that are okay to use to insert content are table elements like <tr> and <td>. The paragraph tag pair denoted by <p> may also contain other content aside from text.

SUMMARY

Sound consists of vibrations that are perpetuated from one medium to another until they reach our eardrums. Understanding technical aspects of digital sound can help us to create smaller sound files without noticeably degrading sound quality. Microphones capture sound and create an analog signal which is converted into a digital signal by sampling the amplitude of the sound wave. For speakers to play a digitized sound, the process is reversed to create an analog signal from the digital sound. There are a number of different formats for digital sound files. In the new HTML5 standard, WAV, MP3, and Ogg are included. This means that web browsers that adhere to the standard will support these sound file formats without additional software installation, like plug-ins. Using sound on a web page can be highly effective at drawing someone's attention to elements on the web page. Sound also has the potential to annoy people and cause web pages to download slowly, so it should be used with care. Sample uses of sound on a web page range from background music to sound effects. Effective use of sound generally makes sounds optional for the user to initiate using a play button.

REFERENCES

Burnie, D. *The concise encyclopedia of the human body*. London: Dorling Kindersley, 1995.
Self, D. *Audio engineering explained: Professional audio recording*. Oxford: Focal, 2009.

CHAPTER TEN

DESIGN: CASCADING STYLE SHEETS AND TEMPLATES

POINTS TO CONSIDER

- What do HTML instructions contribute to a web page?
- What do CSS instructions contribute to a web page?
- What design goals can CSS instructions help achieve?
- What options does one have for embedding CSS instructions into a web page?
- Which CSS embedding option is most useful for sharing design specifications between web pages?

- What is a template?
- What elements of the look and feel of a website can be embedded in a template that cannot be part of a CSS specification?
- How do Amaya templates differ from Adobe Dreamweaver templates?

INTRODUCTION

This text emphasizes developing web pages using software that allows web developers to create web pages without directly specifying HTML instructions. Web pages are actually comprised of two languages, Hypertext Markup Language (HTML) and Cascading Style Sheets (CSS). HTML addresses content and structural aspects of a web page by identifying text, headings, links and multimedia elements that comprise a web page. CSS, on the other hand, addresses the look and feel of a web page, including colors, fonts, and spacing. Understanding some basic concepts pertaining to CSS can make creating a consistent look and feel for a website easier.

While CSS can propagate certain design elements from one web page to another and help avoid having to specify these elements repeatedly on each web page, it cannot propagate all elements that contribute to a website's look and feel, like a common navigation mechanism, logo, header, or other content present on each page in a website.

There is another mechanism, called a template, that can propagate these additional elements from one web page to another.

This chapter will address CSS as its first topic. CSS will be briefly introduced as a computer language, and then strategies for using CSS without programming will be discussed next.

CASCADING STYLE SHEETS (CSS)

In Chapter Six a well-designed website was described as having a consistent look and feel, so this can be accomplished by having each web page that makes up a web site share certain design elements. CSS information can be embedded within the HTML file defining a web page, or this style information can be separated into a file that is linked to multiple web pages. Having CSS information in a separate file makes propagating the look and feel of a website easier. There are three options for adding CSS information to a web page. The CSS can be:

1. in a separate file;
2. applied to categories of HTML elements (internal) or
3. applied to individual HTML elements (inline).

CSS is a computer programming language distinct from HTML. We will briefly look at certain elements of syntax for both CSS and HTML in order to illustrate how they work together. This chapter does not emphasize programming, so a means to harness CSS without writing CSS instructions will be provided.

A Brief Look at CSS Syntax

Figure 10.1 shows a screenshot of Amaya showing a portion of a web page in addition to a portion of the HTML (source) that makes up this page. Recall that the HTML can be viewed in Amaya for a web page by selecting *Views → Show source* from the Amaya menu. In the figure, lines fifteen and seventeen show the HTML that creates the two headings on the web page, "Recommended Hikes in the" and "White Mountains." The <h1> and </h1> are the begin and end tags, respectively, for the headings. The tags identify the type of HTML element and delineate the beginning and ending of the content. Lines eight and ten contain the begin and end tags for an area for CSS instructions. The tags <style> and </style> identify CSS instructions that pertain to various HTML elements. Thus, CSS and HTML work in concert with each other to define the content and look and feel of a web page. The CSS instruction shown in Figure 10.1 on line nine specifies style information for all *h1* elements. The style information in the example specifies that the text should be

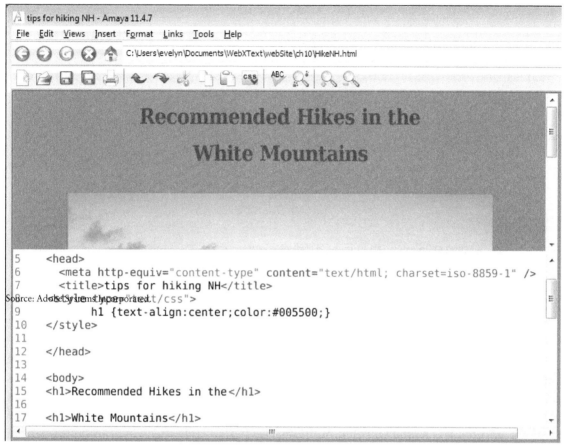

FIGURE 10.1 Amaya screenshot illustrating HTML and CSS
Source: W3C / INRIA.

centered (text-align:center) in the web page and should take on the color defined by the hexadecimal number, 005500. As discussed in Chapter Five, the color code defines the value for the levels of red, green, and blue (RGB) that make up a particular color. The first two digits (00) indicate the amount of red. The second two digits (55) determine the level of green, while the last two digits specify the quantity of blue the color contains.

In the example in Figure 10.1, one can see that the syntax differs between CSS and HTML, yet these two computer languages work together to define a web page. The CSS instructions are located in the style section of the HTML in this example, and thus the style information pertains to all *h1* elements defined to this web page. Alternatively, CSS instructions can be embedded inside a specific HTML tag, and thus pertain only to that element. For example, if we wished to override the default font size for the largest headers only for the first line of heading, the following line could replace line number fifteen in Figure 10.1.

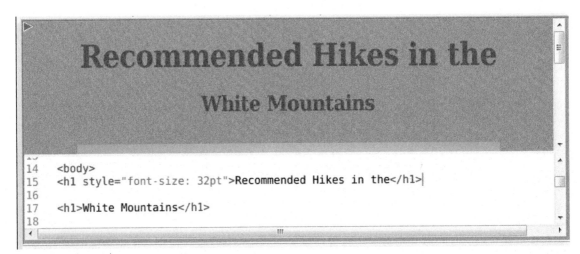

FIGURE 10.2 Embedding style information in an HTML element
Source: W3C / INRIA.

<h1 style="font-size: 32pt">Recommended Hikes in the</h1>

The result of this update is shown in Figure 10.2. One can see that the first line of the heading is significantly larger than the second line of the heading. This example illustrates the use of an inline style, because the style applies only to one HTML element, rather than all *h1* headings. This also illustrates the idea of having cascading style specifications. The term *cascading* refers to the fact that multiple, conflicting style specifications could pertain to the same content on a web page. Cascading suggests that there is an established order of precedence to determine which style information will ultimately be applied to the content. In this example the inline style information overrides the internal style specification.

In order to create a consistent look and feel for the entire website, it is useful to extract the CSS style information and create a separate file that can be referenced by each web page comprising a website. Coding CSS instructions directly is beyond the scope of this text, but this chapter will discuss how to create CSS instructions by using Amaya's graphic interface.

USING CSS IN AMAYA

When one uses Amaya to create web pages, CSS instructions are automatically inserted into the HTML files associated with each page. Figure 10.3 illustrates where one can specify style information in the Amaya interface. The menu item *Format* contains a list of options that pertain to style information. Another means to provide this style information

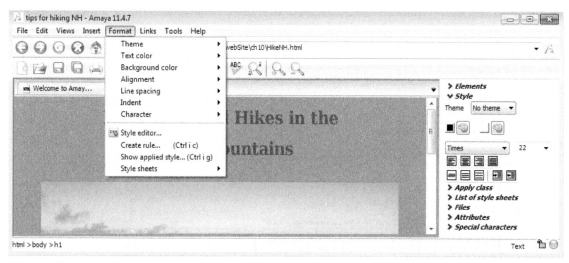

Means to specify style/CSS information using Amaya
Source: W3C / INRIA.

is located on the right-hand side of the Amaya interface under the *Style* option. Style information includes font, font size, text color, background color, alignment, indentation, and theme. Themes are pre-defined styles and Amaya currently provides two themes, *modern* and *classic*. Selecting one of these themes may interfere with creating the look and feel that you have in mind, so you may wish to develop your own look before choosing a theme for your website.

Additional options that one can see in Figure 10.3 under the *Format* menu option are the *Style editor, Create rule ..., Show applied style* and *Style sheets*. The style editor allows advanced style specification, like italics, font weight, boxes around content, blinking text, and text strike-through, to mention a few. The *create rule* option creates CSS instructions that pertain to all elements in a particular category of HTML element (for example, *h1* headings). The *show applied style* option will display the current CSS information for a selected HTML element. Finally, the *style sheets* option allows linking a web page to a file containing CSS instructions. Creating CSS files is a good strategy for establishing a consistent look and feel for a web site. An example of creating a style sheet in Amaya follows.

Creating Style Sheets With Amaya

There are a number of ways to create style sheets using Amaya. A style sheet is a file that contains CSS instructions. One way to create a style sheet is to enter CSS instructions in a file by using the menu option *File → New → New style sheet*. This option requires knowledge of CSS syntax and is beyond the scope of this text. Another means to create a

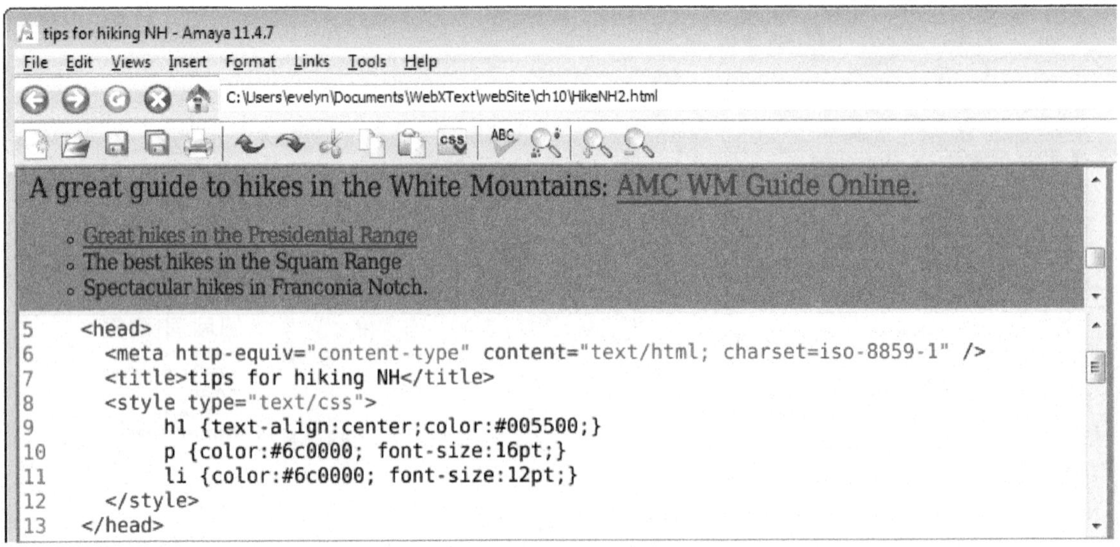

FIGURE 10.4 Capturing style sheet information in Amaya
Source: W3C / INRIA.

style sheet using Amaya entails using the *create rule* option under the *Format* menu item and copying the CSS instructions into a CSS file. When a formatting rule is created while using Amaya, it is recorded in the style section of the HTML file, as shown in Figure 10.4. The CSS instructions are in lines nine through eleven in the figure, and is delineated by the HTML start and end tags, <style> and </style>, respectively. This example provides CSS information for three HTML element types, *h1*, *p*, and *li*. The symbol *h1* stands for the largest heading type, as previously discussed. The character *p* stands for paragraph and identifies areas on a web page containing regular text, as opposed to a heading. The symbol *li* stands for list, and represents an element in a list.

One can copy lines nine through eleven to a new file using Amaya's *File→ New→ New style sheet* menu options, and save the file with a .css file extension. The style sheet file can now be used with other web pages that are to share formatting information. In order to link to a style sheet, select the menu options *Format → Style sheets → Link*, as shown in Figure 10.5. In response to the menu selections, a dialog box will appear that requires the entry of a style sheet file. The result of linking to a CSS file called hikeNH.css is also shown in Figure 10.5, in line eleven. The CSS file can now be used by other pages at this website, allowing easy replication of format information.

CSS formatting information can also be created in Adobe Dreamweaver. This topic will be broached next.

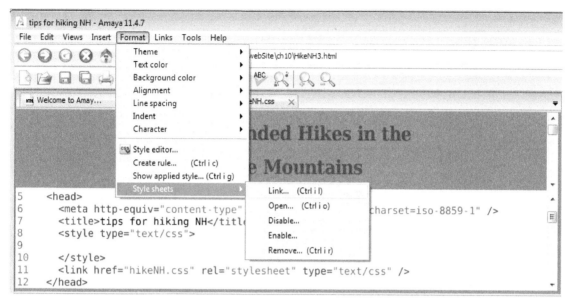

FIGURE 10.5 Linking to a style sheet using Amaya
Source: W3C / INRIA.

USING CSS WITH ADOBE DREAMWEAVER

Creating style sheets in Adobe Dreamweaver is similar to creating style sheets in Amaya. One can create a CSS file directly by selecting the menu options *File → New … → CSS* and then pressing the *Create* button. In addition to directly entering CSS instructions into the file, Dreamweaver provides a menu-driven approach to creating style sheets. Because CSS syntax is beyond the scope of this text and the menu-driven approach is relatively complex, these options will not be further explored. Instead a brief overview of the Dreamweaver interface will be provided, emphasizing elements of CSS.

The Dreamweaver interface makes a distinction between HTML and CSS. Figure 10.6 shows the property window in HTML mode on top and CSS mode in the bottom portion of the figure. One may toggle between CSS and HTML by using the buttons on the left-hand side of the window. The HTML properties allow the specification of a variety of text formats, including six sizes of headings using the *Format* pull-down menu. Some additional formatting information can be specified here, including bold/italics and bulleted lists.

The Page Properties button at the bottom of both HTML and CSS mode property windows is useful for specifying formats that pertain to the entire web page. Figure 10.7 illustrates the page properties window. There is a list of categories of properties on the left-hand side of the window. Several properties are denoted as either HTML or CSS. Because

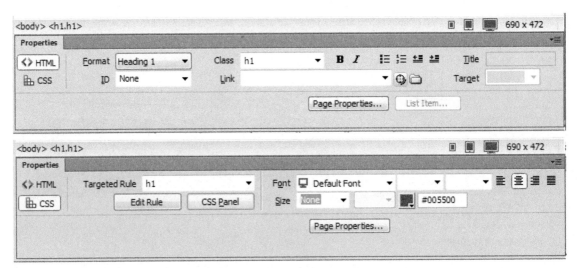

FIGURE 10.6 The HTML and CSS modes of the property window
Source: Adobe Systems Incorporated.

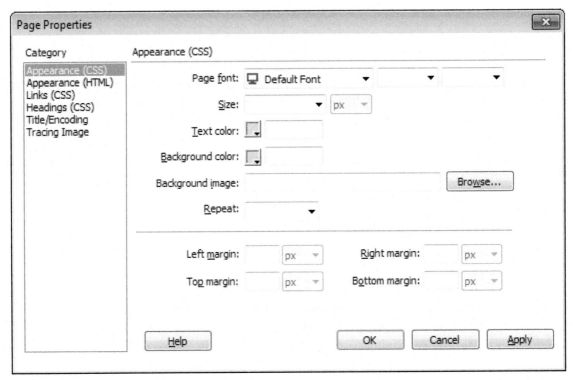

FIGURE 10.7 Adobe Dreamweaver's Page Properties window
Source: Adobe Systems Incorporated.

the properties pertain to the entire web page, selected CSS properties create entries in the style section of the HTML header as follows:

```
<style type="text/css">
 body { font-family: Impact, Haettenschweiler, "Franklin
    Gothic Bold", "Arial Black", sans-serif;
 color: #339966; }
</style>
```

The above CSS instructions specify the font type and color for the entire web page. This information can then be extracted and saved in a CSS file to be used by other web pages.

Figure 10.6 shows a text field labeled *Class* in the upper portion of the figure. This mechanism facilitates the definition of a class of HTML elements that can be assigned the same CSS properties. These class-wide property definitions are created in the style section of the HTML header section, like the page-wide property definitions. These CSS definitions can be copied into a CSS file and then used by multiple web pages.

In addition to web page-wide or class-wide CSS definitions, these definitions can be made in-line. An in-line CSS definition assigns the CSS properties to the selected HTML element only. In order to assign properties to a limited area, one would select the desired HTML element and then select <*New Inline Style*> from the *Targeted Rule* text field, as can be seen in the lower portion of Figure 10.6. Next, one would select the desired properties to be applied to the HTML element.

There are more advanced CSS properties that one may use to format HTML elements beyond the properties available in the window shown in Figure 10.6. Figure 10.8 shows the text-shadow property available in the properties section of the CSS designer window. The result of applying a text shadow is also illustrated. The CSS designer can be opened using the *Window* menu item and then selecting *CSS Designer*, or by pressing the *CSS Panel* button in the CSS properties window.

The look and feel of a web site goes beyond the format information encoded in style sheets. It includes things like common navigation buttons, headers, logos, or other widgets. Another mechanism that allows the sharing of these additional look and feel features is the template.

USING TEMPLATES

Templates are files that contain common web page elements that are to be shared by pages comprising a website. Both Amaya and Adobe Dreamweaver support templates.

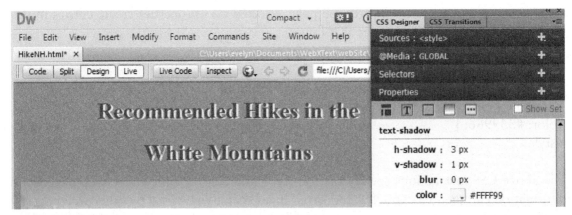

FIGURE 10.8 Advanced formatting using Adobe Dreamweaver
Source: Adobe Systems Incorporated.

It is important to keep in mind that templates are not a standard web element, but are rather mechanisms specific to a web development tool. Templates created in Amaya are not compatible with Dreamweaver and templates created in Dreamweaver are not compatible with Amaya. Thus, templates are unlike anything that has been discussed so far, because other web elements created so far are compatible with any web page editor. The basic approach of templates is similar between Amaya and Dreamweaver. Amaya will be addressed first.

Templates in Amaya

Amaya currently provides two predefined templates that may be used to create web pages. It also supports the creation of new templates. In order to create a template, one should create a web page consisting of the areas that are to be common to all web pages using this template. For example, one could create a template that contains the background and text colors of the web site in addition to the header image and navigation buttons, as shown in Figure 10.9. This figure also illustrates how to create a template from this web page.

When one wishes to create a new web page using a template, the template file can be specified during the web page creation process. Figure 10.10 shows the window that is displayed in response to selecting the menu options *File → New document*. This window has a check box labeled *From template*. When this box is checked one can specify a template file. Note that the file extension for template files is .xtd. When one creates a web page from a template, the information contained in the template file is transmitted to the new web page. The web page developers can then add content to the initial template information.

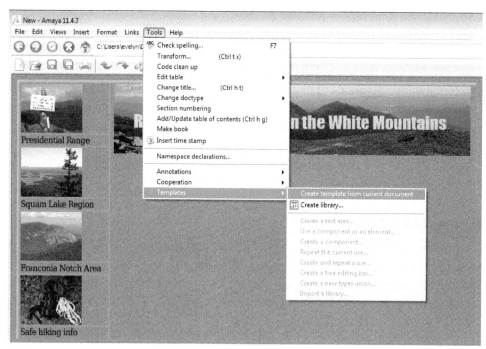

FIGURE 10.9 A possible template for the hiking website
Source: W3C / INRIA.

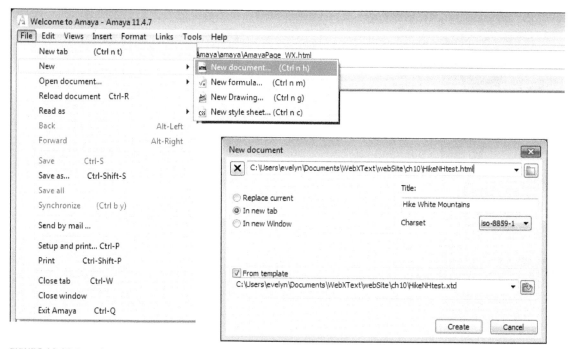

FIGURE 10.10 Creating a web page from a template
Source: W3C / INRIA.

This approach is structurally similar to the iframe approach discussed in Chapter Six, because the header and navigation mechanisms are held constant from one web page to another. The difference between using iframes and templates to propagate design information is that iframes use the same URL to present a potentially wide range of information, whereas templates use distinct URLs for each web page. Thus, when someone searches for a piece of information on a website using iframes, a specific URL cannot be associated with this information. In contrast, a similar website using templates can associate a unique URL with each page.

Templates in Dreamweaver are similar to templates in Amaya, and will be briefly explored next.

Templates in Adobe Dreamweaver

The basic approach to using templates in Adobe Dreamweaver is the same as in Amaya. One creates a template file that embodies the common elements among a group of web pages to be created. Figure 10.11 illustrates how a template can be created using the *Insert →Template → Make Template* menu options. A template file is created in

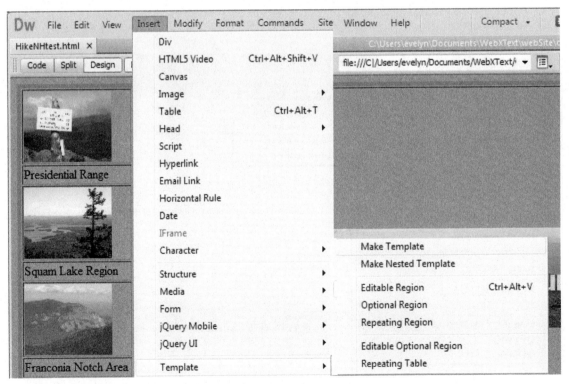

FIGURE 10.11 Creating a template using Adobe Dreamweaver
Source: Adobe Systems Incorporated.

response to this sequence of selections. Template files created using Dreamweaver have a .dwt file extension.

There are some important differences in Dreamweaver's management of templates in contrast to how Amaya manages templates. Dreamweaver manages the use of templates by preventing the modification of any elements that are part of the template after the template has been used to create a web page. The only areas that can be modified in the new web page are in the *editable regions* of the template. Figure 10.11 shows the menu options available for templates, including the *Editable Region* option. Dreamweaver also allows the modification of the template itself after it has been applied to the creation of web pages. Dreamweaver applies the template modification to the web pages that have been created from the changed template. For example, if there is another category of hikes to be added along with a corresponding thumbnail image in the table of linked images, this image would be added to all web pages that used this template. Amaya does not manage the use of templates in this manner, so such updates to templates must be manually carried out.

SUMMARY

Web pages have been described as being defined by HTML. In fact, web pages are defined by two computer programming languages that work in concert with each other, HTML and CSS. HTML can be generally characterized as the web page definition language that determines what text, hyperlinks, and multimedia elements comprise a web page. HTML also determines the layout for these elements. CSS, on the other hand, determines things like fonts, font sizes, colors, and indentation. There are some options for using CSS in a web page definition. CSS can be applied to an individual web element or to a category of elements. If the CSS specification is applied to a category of web elements, the specification can be defined in a web page HTML file or in a separate CSS file. The advantage of using a separate CSS file is that it can be shared by multiple web pages to contribute to a consistent look and feel.

Templates are another means to capture essential elements of web page design. In addition to embodying the essential design elements of CSS, templates can also contain web elements that are to be common among a series of web pages. Unlike the topics discussed so far pertaining to HTML and CSS, templates are not standardized. This means that a template defined in Amaya will not function with web pages defined in Adobe Dreamweaver and vice versa.

CHAPTER ELEVEN

VIDEO

POINTS TO CONSIDER

- What complexities exist when using video on a website?
- What ethical considerations exist pertaining to the use of video on the web?
- What is the WAI?
- What suggestions does the WAI make regarding video content on the web?
- What ethical concerns pertain to image maps?
- How can one enhance the operability of image maps?
- What ethical issues are relevant to video content?
- What design considerations exist regarding adding video to a web page?

- What video file formats are commonly supported by web browsers?
- How can one address the situation that different web browsers support different video file formats?
- How can one reduce the size of a video file?
- What trade-offs are there for each strategy for video file size reduction?
- What are the strengths and weaknesses of Windows Movie Maker?
- How can one keep video file sizes small using Windows Movie Maker?

INTRODUCTION

Video is a popular form of media on the Internet; however there are complexities in using video as a means to communicate information or entertain your audience. One obvious problem with video is the amount of data that must be transmitted over the Internet in order to download or stream a video file. Video files are like frame-based animations in that they consist of a sequence of images shown in quick succession. In Chapter Five individual images were discussed as potentially contributing to long download times, so video content is of much greater concern than individual images, since a video file can consist of hundreds or thousands of images. Video file sizes are influenced by a number of factors, such as the size of the video (its dimensions), the length of the video (how many minutes/seconds it runs), the resolution of the video, the frame rate (how many frames per second are shown), and color bit depth. Depending on the software used for creating a video, one may or may not have control over certain factors influencing its file size.

Aside from contributing to slow download times, a series of other considerations exist with the use of video. Another problem with video content is that individuals with visual disabilities may not be able to appreciate it, so an alternate form of this content should be made available. Another challenge with creating video content for the web is that sophisticated video editing software can be expensive to acquire. Fortunately, there are free, easy-to-use video creation tools available on computers running popular operating systems, such as those that run on Macintosh and PC-compatible computers. The video tool available with the Windows operating system will be explored further in this chapter. In addition to introducing readers to a freely available video creation tool, other design considerations will be explored. This chapter will commence by exploring ethical considerations of using video on a website.

ETHICS OF VIDEO USE ON THE WEB

There are a number of factors that prompt ethical considerations when it comes to using video on a website. One consideration involves access to the information or experience embodied in the video. One's access could be limited due to a visual or auditory impairment, or one could have difficulty accessing video content as a result of slow Internet connection speeds. In either case, an alternate form of the content should be provided. Another important area for ethical reflection pertains to the content of the video. This ethical category understandably overlaps with the ethics of image use on the web, as previously discussed in this text.

Accessibility of Video Content

There are a number of guidelines published by the Web Accessibility Initiative (WAI) that are relevant to this chapter. The WAI is orchestrated under the larger World Wide Web Consortium (W3C) organization, which is the international body that oversees standards for the web. The primary accessibility principles of interest here are that content is *perceivable* and *operable* by everyone. These guidelines can be found here http://www.w3.org/WAI/intro/people-use-web/principles (Abou-Zahra 2012). A few WAI suggestions will be elaborated upon next.

For a video to be perceivable by someone with either an auditory or visual impairment, the WAI recommends a text alternative. For the visually impaired, a text alternative allows a screen reading device to translate the text into speech. A text alternative for a still image might consist of a caption or the use of the *alternate text* field. The alternate text field can be specified when one adds an image to a web page using either Amaya or Adobe Dreamweaver. The HTML5 standard is evolving to use a more extensive text area, called the *Image Description Extension*, which uses the *longdesc* HTML tag. Images can include things like buttons, logos, graphic headers, or other graphics and conventional images. The purpose of the text is to provide an equivalent experience by describing the purpose of the image along with information conveyed by the image. Because videos tend to be more substantial than individual images, a longer text equivalent is generally necessary. The text could include a transcript of the video's narrative content as well as descriptions of imagery.

A video's operability can be enhanced if it does not require a mouse to operate. Individuals who are visually impaired are less likely to be able to use video controls that require mouse operation. Fortunately, video players can be controlled using keyboard keys instead of a mouse, and therefore video players adhere to the principle of operability. Another aspect of operability includes not having video content that might induce seizures. This suggests that videos should not contain flashing content. Despite adhering to these operability principles, the content playing in the video player may not be adequately accessible, so an alternative form of content, like a text-based description of the content, is still in order.

Figure 11.1 illustrates an element of the hiking web site that should be modified to enhance accessibility. The traffic light with the color-coded words is an image map. Each light of the traffic light and an associated word serve as a hotspot to link to a web page with hikes of the specified difficulty level. It should be noted that the words in the image

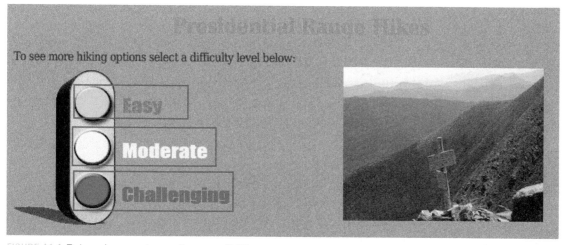

FIGURE 11.1 Enhancing a web page's accessibility

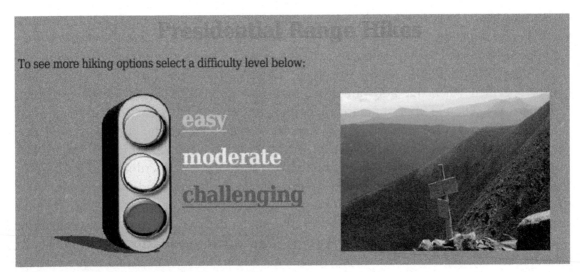

FIGURE 11.2 A more operable version of the image map

map are part of the image, as opposed to text. Although the hotspots of an image map can be selected using the tab key, thereby enhancing operability, the arrangement of hotspots is likely to be confusing to an individual who is visually impaired. Although each image map hotspot can have alternate text associated with it, not all web page editors prompt for this feature.

Figure 11.2 shows a slight variation to the image map shown in Figure 11.1, to enhance operability of the site. Instead of using an image map alone, a column of links can be added, as shown in Figure 11.2. In order to recreate the visual effect of the previous figure, the words "easy," "moderate," and "challenging" were removed from the image and recreated as a column of heading-sized text-based links. The hotspots were also recreated so that they cover only the light area. The hotspot areas, shown as blue rectangles or circles, do not appear on the actual web page, but are shown in the figures to show the change in hotspot coverage.

The Americans with Disabilities Act (ADA) (1990) requires that web page content can be usable by people with disabilities. In addition to this legal mandate, it is ethical to consider the needs of as wide an audience as possible during web page design.

Other Ethical Considerations

We live in an age in which video recording is almost ubiquitous. Anyone carrying a cell phone is carrying a video recording device. Also, many public and corporate spaces are being recorded by video cameras. Recording may occur anywhere, from a Walmart parking lot to a city street. The purpose of a video recording could be to capture evidence of a potential crime, a happy experience, how-to material for do-it-yourself projects, or a newsworthy event.

Many ethical considerations for video content mirror those for still images. In that spirit, a video should not violate the privacy of others, show gratuitous violence, misrepresent reality, or reinforce stereotypes. It should be considerate to the victims of crime or disaster. So, before posting a video on a web page, the individuals shown in the video should consent to their presence in the video to protect their right to privacy.

Although gratuitous violence should be avoided, how does one handle the reporting of a gory or violent incident? There are competing objectives when including video recordings of disasters or crime scenes. One wishes to be sensitive to the victims of such incidents and yet still convey the severity of such situations. Also, the source of the video should be considered. For example, one should not show a video from a terrorist group showing a terrifying act, because distributing this video helps the terrorists terrorize the public.

Just as one can edit an image to misrepresent reality, like darkening O.J. Simpson's mug shot, videos can be edited to misrepresent a situation. Political ads are famous for using such tactics. One key video editing technique is to take a phrase out of context to suggest the person said something quite different from what he or she intended to say. One famous incident involves the firing of Shirley Sherrod, Georgia State Director of Rural Development for the United States Department of Agriculture, as a result of a video posted at a conservative website. A speech she gave to the NAACP was recorded and edited to make it appear as if Ms. Sherrod, who is African American, indicated that she would not assist white farmers. She, in fact, said the opposite, and received an apology from the White House with an offer to reinstate her (Stolberg 2010).

Distorting reality through video editing can be acceptable if it is for comic or artistic effect, and if it is clear that the video is not meant to represent reality. Another popular digital editing technique is called a *mashup*, and involves taking snippets from a series of videos to create a new aggregate video or using the sound track of one video to apply to cuts of another video. *Fifty Shades of Green* (Swofford 2014) is an example of a popular mashup in which scenes from the *Muppet Movie* are dubbed with dialogue from *Fifty Shades of Grey*.

Finally, stereotyping merits discussion beyond what was discussed in Chapter Five. One should avoid portraying unflattering generalizations about groups of people, whether in still images or videos. These groups can be identified by common race, ethnicity, gender, sexual identification or preference, age, ability, religion, and so on. Images and videos have the potential of discriminating against groups of people by omission as well. For example, on the NH hiking website, if all hiking videos showed young, white, able-bodied men hiking, this would communicate that hiking is not meant for women, disabled people, older people, or people not belonging to the dominant racial demographic. On a small-scale website, it is probably difficult to find hiking videos that cover the full spectrum of diversity, but a reasonable effort should be made.

Certain ethical considerations pertaining to video have design implications, particularly accessibility. The next section explores other design issues pertaining to using video on a website.

DESIGN

Design considerations pertaining to video content on the web fall into two categories: video design and website design. The section will start by addressing website design.

Website Design

When adding video to a website, one must be mindful of people with slower-speed Internet connections. Video should be included on a web page so that it does not automatically play, but is rather played at the discretion of the viewer. To adhere to the HTML5 standard for video, one should make the controls for a video player available so that users can elect to view the video or not. Having available controls would also address the concern about timed media playing too quickly for some individuals, and thereby allow selected portions of the video to be replayed. While the HTML5 standard does not require specific video file formats, the W3C standards organization recommends video formats that do not have patents requiring royalties. Because one cannot guarantee a specific video file format will be supported by a web browser, the HTML5 video standard sets up a fallback structure. The fallback mechanism allows a sequence of video files to be specified. If the first video file format is not supported by the web browser, it attempts to play the second. If the second video file format is not supported, a third video file is attempted. If none of the video file formats are supported by the web browser, a message is shown. A sample HTML5 video instruction is shown below.

```
<video poster="hikeVideo.jpg" controls>
       <source src="hikeVideo.mp4" type="video/mp4" >
       <source src="hikeVideo.webm" type="video/webm" >
       <source src="hikeVideo.ogv" type="video/ogg">
       <p>Your Browser does not support this video format</p>
</video>
```

Figure 11.3 illustrates how video can be added using Adobe Dreamweaver. The *Insert* menu item allows the selection of *HTML5 Video*. When this video format is selected, the properties window allows the specification of the video file in addition to two alternate video files, using the fallback mechanism described in the preceding paragraph. There is

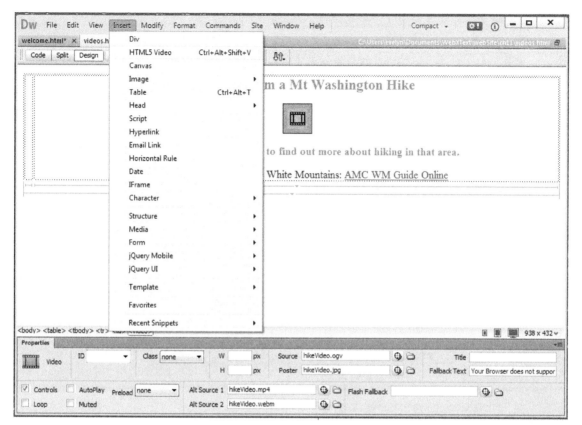

FIGURE 11.3 Adding video using Adobe Dreamweaver
Source: Adobe Systems Incorporated.

also a text field, labeled *Fallback Text*, that allows for the specification of a message that will display should the web browser not support any of the specified video file formats. Note the *Controls* checkbox in the lower left-hand corner of the figure adds the word "controls" in the first line of the video instruction. This adds video controls to the video player in the web page, as previously recommended. A final video property identified in the figure is the *Poster* text field. This text field contains the file name "hikeVideo.jpg," which identifies the image that should be shown in the video player.

Figure 11.4 shows the web page with the video player defined by the sample video instructions. The dimensions of the player are determined by the dimensions of the poster image, unless otherwise specified. These dimensions could be overridden by specifying a width and height in the video property window shown in Figure 11.3. The controls at the bottom of the video player allow the user to view the video electively. The controls also indicate the length of the video, forty-four seconds in this case. The length of the video gives an indication as to the general size of the video file to be downloaded.

FIGURE 11.4 Sample video player on a web page

The video formats listed in the sample HTML5 instruction list three common video file formats. According to Robbins (2012), these video file formats have the following characteristics.

- MP4 (Moving Pictures Expert Group-4) serves as a container format for H.264 format video and ACC audio format. H.264 is a high-quality video format, but is patented and must be licensed for a fee. The required royalty has prevented many web browsers from supporting it.
- Ogg is a container format for the Theora video format with the Vorbis audio format. The quality of this format is considered to be inferior to the other video formats, but it is royalty-free, so web browsers readily support this format.
- WebM serves as a container format for the VP8 video format and the Vorbis audio format. It is open-source and royalty-free, so can be readily used in web browsers.

Other possible video formats include formats associated with the popular computer operating systems Windows and Mac OS.

- Wmv—Windows Media Video is the video format originally produced for the MS Windows operating system and is a proprietary format. With the establishment of the HTML5 standard, Windows Movie Maker, Microsoft's free video creation tool, creates MP4 video files in addition to wmv files.
- Mov—is Apple's Quicktime video file format and was produced for the Mac OS.
- Avi—Audio Video Interleave is an MS Windows standard format.
- Flv—is a video format used by Adobe Flash to encapsulate MPEG video.

Unless the web server has video streaming capabilities, videos are downloaded as a whole. Clearly, video file size is an important consideration when using such content on the web. The next section explores strategies for reducing file size.

CREATING EFFICIENT VIDEOS FOR THE WEB

In Chapter Five, strategies were provided to create efficient image files. The most effective strategy for keeping image files small was to reduce the dimensions of the image. Because videos consist of a series of images shown in rapid succession, strategies for creating efficient image file sizes are also important for creating efficient video file sizes. If individual images can produce slow web page download times, it is even more important to keep video files as small as possible. The strategies for reducing video file sizes can be summarized as follows.

- Video length—The number of seconds/minutes a video plays has a significant influence on the overall file size. The relationship between video playing time and file size will be explored in the context of Windows Movie Maker in the next section.
- Frame size—The size of the frame identifies the dimensions of the images being encoded, so this will also have a significant influence on the video file size. This relationship will be further illustrated in the next section as well. If the video is too small, critical details may be missed by the viewer, however.
- Frame resolution—The resolution of a frame relates directly to its dimensions, but a lower-resolution frame can be stretched to a larger frame size. If one reduces the resolution too much, then a poor-quality video can result.
- Frame rate—If one keeps the overall play time constant and one reduces the number of frames that are played per second, this will reduce the video file size. The consequence of reducing the frame rate too much is a jumpy video. The higher the frame rate, the smoother the video.
- Color depth—This strategy was discussed in Chapter Five as a means to reduce image size. So, if the size of each frame is reduced by recording fewer bits for each color, the video file size can be significantly reduced. An excessively small color depth could result in distorted colors, however.

The next section looks at creating simple videos using Windows Movie Maker. In this section strategies for keeping video file sizes as small as possible will also be explored.

USING WINDOWS MOVIE MAKER

Both Apple and Windows operating systems have free video development tools. As free products, they have limited capabilities, but are still a handy option for web content. This section explores using Windows Movie Maker.

Movie Maker is a good tool for splicing together still images and video snippets. One use for Movie Maker is to create a slide show with narration. Using Windows Movie Maker, one can specify the timing each image should show, apply captions and visual effects to each image, and select animated transitions between images. Movie Maker provides several visual effects that are applied to individual images, like adding tones, changing a color

FIGURE 11.5 Windows Movie Maker interface
Source: Microsoft.

image to black and white, applying various cinematic overlays, and so on. There are also a number of animated transitions between slides that one may select to make the still images seem more dynamic. Movie Maker supports the recording of narration or other sound effects as well as the insertion of a sound track.

Figure 11.5 shows the Movie Maker interface with a series of still images. The most difficult aspect of creating a video is planning the video and assembling the raw materials. Once this is complete, adding a title, credits, videos, images, captions, effects, transitions, music, and narration is extremely easy. Movie Maker allows the movie to be previewed in the area on the left-hand side of the interface to assist with adjusting the timing of elements of the video. When one saves the Movie Maker project file, the raw elements, like images, video, and sound, are not part of the Movie Maker project file, which has a .wlmp file extension. So, if one moves the project file, one must move these resources with it to keep the project intact.

In order to create a video file that can be included on a web page, one must save the movie. Movie Maker supports the creation of two video file formats, *wmv* and *MP4*. The MP4 video format is more apt to be supported by web browsers than the wmv format. As one creates a video file, one also specifies the destination of the video, thereby influencing the video size. Some options for video file destination are high-definition display, DVD, computer, email, iPhone, Android phone, tablet, Facebook, YouTube, and so on. One would anticipate that the file size of a video created for a high-definition display would be significantly larger than one created for email.

TABLE 11.1 File sizes for a forty-second video saved with different preferences in Movie Maker

VIDEO FORMAT	COMPUTER	HIGH DEFINITION	EMAIL	FACEBOOK	YOUTUBE	IPHONE
MP4	2 MB	10 MB	.67 MB	5.7 MB	10 MB	5.7 MB
wmv	4 MB	11.4 MB	1.5 MB	7 MB	11.5 MB	6.9 MB

Table 11.1 illustrates the file sizes for different movie save options in Movie Maker for a video made from nine images playing for four seconds each, along with a four-second title screen. Thus, the video plays for forty seconds. The variation in file sizes between each option results primarily from the image resolutions used in the video. The high-definition video is significantly larger than the one created for e-mail. One can also see from Table 11.1 that the file sizes for .mp4 videos are about half that of the .wmv videos. This suggests that MP4 videos are more suitable for web deployment.

When the overall video length is cut in half by reducing the amount of time each image is shown, the file size is also cut in half. The nature of this video is to repeat video frames with the exact same content for four seconds in one case and two seconds in the next. Because the file size reduction directly correlates to the length reduction, there appears to be no compression across frames. That is, despite significant repetition of content from one frame to the next, each frame seems to be encoded in its entirety. The same relationship between video length and file size holds true for either .mp4 or .wmv format video files. This suggests that when developing video content for the web, it is advisable to design the video carefully to create a video that accomplishes its goal with the fewest frames. The other significant design consideration that one may deduce from Table 11.1 is that, as long as the picture quality is acceptable, one should select as low a resolution as possible. Because Windows Movie Maker is a free product with the Windows operating system, its versatility is limited, so one has limited control over the options contributing to video file size.

SUMMARY

Video content can be a wonderful asset on the web when used carefully. Web users are accustomed to readily available video content, so video seems like a necessary option for conveying some content. One must be aware of individuals who have slow Internet connection speeds or who have impairments that make appreciating video content difficult or impossible. So, videos should be played at the discretion of the viewer, and text-based alternatives should be provided. In addition to considerations concerning the accessibility of video content, there are ethical considerations that address the nature of the video content. These concerns relate to ensuring the veracity of the content, protecting the privacy of others, protecting victims of crime or disaster, being cautious when portraying violent or gruesome content, and avoiding stereotypes.

Because videos consume significant network resources, steps should be taken to keep them as small as possible. The most effective approach to creating efficient videos is to plan the content carefully so that one communicates one's message efficiently. The length of the video is directly proportional to its file size, so video playing time should be kept as short as possible. Other design steps that one can take are to reduce the frame size, reduce the frame rate, use a smaller bit depth for the color, and reduce the resolution.

Finally, video editing tools can be expensive to acquire. Fortunately, there are free tools available with popular operating systems. These free tools have limited functionality, but are nonetheless useful under certain circumstances. Windows Movie Maker is looked at in this chapter.

REFERENCES

Abou-Zahra, S. "Accessibility Principles." http://www.w3.org/WAI/intro/people-use-web/principles, 2012.

Americans with Disabilities Act of 1990. http://www.ada.gov/pubs/adastatute08.htm, 1990.

Robbins, J. *Learning Web Design, A beginner's Guide to HTML, CSS, Javascript and Web Graphics.* Sebastopol, CA: O'Reilly Media, Inc., 2012.

Stolberg, S. (2010) "White House Apologizes to Shirley Sherrod," *New York Times*, July 21, 2010, http://www.nytimes.com/2010/07/22/us/politics/22sherrod.html.

Swofford, B. "Fifty Shades of Green." (2014) The Trailer Mash, Movie trailers recut. August 25, 2014. http://www.thetrailermash.com/fifty-shades-of-green-romance/.

CHAPTER TWELVE

BLOGGING: CITIZEN JOURNALISM

POINTS TO CONSIDER

- What is the blogosphere?
- What distinguishes a blog from a regular website?
- How did blogging begin?
- What kinds of blogs exist?
- What motivates people to blog?
- What kind of rewards are there for bloggers?
- How can one find interesting blogs to follow?

- What are two incidents in which bloggers influenced the coverage of news in the mainstream media?
- What are some typical elements of a blog?
- Where can one set up a blog without cost?
- What rules of netiquette apply to blogging?

INTRODUCTION

The Blogosphere is the subset of the World Wide Web that is comprised of weblogs, otherwise known as blogs. Blogs are a special form of web page that contain periodic chronological entries in a diary-like manner (Blood 2002). Blogs often allow readers to leave comments on a particular blog entry, and blog authors may respond to readers' comments, creating a dialogue. Another characteristic that distinguishes blogs from other web pages is that they are easy to create. Any person who has moderate to high-speed access to the Internet can create a blog free of charge with easy-to-use software at a variety of blogging websites, like blogger.com, wordpress.com, or livejournal.com. The need for access to the Internet in order to blog suggests that blogging exacerbates the digital divide, and provides another occasion where poor and rural citizens lack a voice (Cauley 2009). Additional obstacles to a digital democracy, beyond Internet connectivity and computer ownership, are technical literacy and time availability/commitment (Davis 1999).

Blogging began in two different forms. One blog form was created by individuals writing online diaries as web pages (Herring, Kouper et al. 2004), while the other blog form began as what is known as filter blogs (Blood 2002). The purpose of filter blogs was to help readers manage the vast volume of information available on the Internet by directing people to particularly useful or interesting websites pertaining to a given topic. Filter blogs consisted of a series of links with annotations to identify the characteristics of a linked-to website. Thus, filter blogs were originally a kind of directory to web content.

Since the origins of blogging, other blog forms have become popular, including blogs that contain original content, known as K-blogs or knowledge blogs (Herring, Kouper et al. 2004). The blogging phenomenon has taken off. According to Technorati's "State of the Blogosphere," 133 million blog entries have been tracked since 2002 (Technorati 2008). The volume of information contained in blogs is so massive that people require directories to help them to find high-quality blogs of interest.

Within the category of knowledge blogs, there is a wide array of content areas. Some major categories for knowledge blogs are politics, living (cooking, home design, etc.), technology, entertainment (TV/movie reviews, celebrity gossip, and so on), sports, business, and journal blogs. So blogging allows individuals to publish information on a wide range of topics very easily. The next section explores other motivations for blogging beyond the ease of doing so.

THE APPEAL OF BLOGS

Before we explore the appeal of blogs, it is useful to establish how blogs differ from regular websites. Their structural differences have been briefly mentioned, in that they contain a sequence of chronological entries and often allow comments, but how does the content differ from a regular website? This answer can be best understood by looking at a concrete example. The content of a New Hampshire hiking website would generally be more static. Once the desired hike, safety, and other information have been established, the site would serve as a reference for those wishing to hike. The information pertaining to a hike would be relatively standard and consist of things like length, difficulty level, elevation gain, river crossings, viewpoints, and other noteworthy features. In contrast, a hiking blog would discuss the experience of hiking in terms of the conditions on the day of the hike. This could consist of the weather, outdoor temperature at the beginning of the hike, temperature at the top of the mountain, how one addressed any challenges of the day (such as river crossings or rock scrambles), the equipment one packed and the food and water consumed on the way, views from the summit, one's feelings at various points along the hike, and people one encounters. Each blog entry would discuss the experience of a hike. The same hiking trail could provide different blog posts, especially if the weather conditions varied between hikes.

The process of blogging can be appealing for a number of reasons. The process of organizing one's thoughts and creating an articulate statement is satisfying in itself. One may be confronting a difficult life experience, and the process of expressing this experience can be therapeutic. Additionally, one may get supportive comments from readers.

Blogging can also be financially rewarding. For example, a popular mommy blogger (someone who blogs about one's experience as a mother), Heather B. Armstrong (Dooce. com), earns enough money from advertisers on her blog that she supports her family by blogging (Armstrong 2014). Other bloggers, such as Ree Drummond (thepioneerwoman. com) became a cookbook author as a result of her popularity as a blogger (Drummond 2014). Ree Drummond now has a cooking show on the Food Network. Many political bloggers have gained mainstream media prominence or have gotten a traditional journalist position. Anna Marie Cox, who founded Wonkette.com in 2004, has held a number of prominent positions as a journalist. Markos Moulitsas Zúniga started the political blog dailykos.com in 2002. He had gained prominence as a political commentator on MSNBC for a period of time. So, blogging can be a springboard for other lucrative opportunities or can be financially rewarding itself.

In order to become known as a blogger, one has to distinguish oneself from millions of other bloggers. In the case of Heather B. Armstrong, she has a very compelling story of postpartum depression in addition to having excellent writing skills and a cutting sense of humor. Her skill as a writer not only led to her role as a popular blogger, but also landed her multiple book deals. This suggests that blogging can provide a means for being discovered as a writer.

How one becomes known as a blogger raises the question of how one's blog is found by interested readers. The next section explores this question.

HOW ARE BLOGS FOUND?

Understanding how blogs are found can help one find highly rated blogs of a desired genre or topic while also providing information about how one's own blog may find a readership. There are a few ways that people find blogs. Blogs can be found as a result of:

- a web search for a topic of interest;
- word of mouth;
- a link from a familiar blog; or
- a blog directory.

A web search could lead to blog readership. For example, if someone has a technical question or is looking for a recipe and searches the web for this information, a blog post may provide the desired result. Reading the post containing the search result could lead to ongoing readership. This approach might work well for certain genres of blogs, like technology, business, or cooking, but less well for blogs that are not knowledge-focused.

An example of a type of blog that is unlikely to surface in a web search is a mommy blog. A mommy blog is a form of journal or diary blog in which women discuss their experiences as mothers. Although some mommy blogs have recipes, like thepioneerwoman.com, and may surface during a search, others, like Dooce.com, do not contain how-to information. One could hear of Dooce through family and friends who may have discovered her or find a link to her blog on another blog. There is another option for discovering blogs: blog directories.

Blog directories are websites that list blogs of a certain type or classify blogs into subject matter-based categories. These directories generally have some means to determine the popularity of each blog and use this to determine how blogs are sequenced. Technorati. com was one of the most influential blog directories, but has recently ceased functioning as a blog directory (Bhuiyan 2014). It can serve as an example of how blog directories are structured. Technorati had a series of blogging categories that evolved over time to reflect current trends in blogging. In 2009 the categories included technology, business, entertainment, lifestyle, sports, and politics. These blog categories left out an important genre of blog, namely journal blogs. Because journal blogs were often omitted by blog directories, and because most journal bloggers are women (Herring, Kouper et al. 2004), blog directories were considered to privilege men over women. To rectify this situation, Blogher.com was started to highlight blogs authored by women.

The next section explores whether blogs have transformed the mainstream media, and therefore society, in any way.

HOW BLOGS ENHANCE INFORMATION EXCHANGE

The mainstream media refer to media sources like television, radio, newspapers, and magazines that have substantial distribution and are therefore run by large organizations like corporations. Most media organizations are for-profit, but some are not-for-profit. These organizations have an editorial process that scrutinizes every story before it is aired or printed. This centralized editorial scrutiny is known as *gatekeeping*. So, an individual who has a newsworthy idea must approach a media outlet and pass through the editorial process before this idea can be aired. Most people do not succeed, or attempt expressing themselves through major media outlets. Blogging, on the other hand, allows individuals to reach the public directly without having to go through such gatekeepers.

Despite excluding critical segments of our society, the blogosphere has been touted as a means to enhance awareness and discussion of important civic matters (Zúniga, Puig-I-Abril et al. 2009). Four means to engage politically through blogs have been identified, including persuading others to agree with one's political perspective (known as *agenda setting*), investigating political subject matter, encouraging an inclusive dialog, and facilitating a direct interaction between politicians and their constituents (Siapera 2008). According to a recent PEW study, bloggers are almost equally split between men and women (Lenhart and Fox 2006), so women are able to express themselves almost on par with men. The blogosphere is regarded as a more democratic forum for the discussion of ideas than the mainstream media because the vast majority of blogs are created by individuals or small groups of individuals, as opposed to media outlets owned and influenced by large corporations (Bagdikian 2000). These characteristics of the blogosphere create a sense of engagement, equity, and accessibility, in contrast to the corporate-owned mainstream media (McChesney and Scott 2004).

Early expectations for the blogosphere were that it would serve as a means for individuals to express ideas to a large audience, thus creating a vibrant civic discourse. In the formative period of the blogosphere, this seemed to be the case, as evidenced by the previously unknown individuals who made names for themselves through blogging. Examples of such individuals are Ana Marie Cox of Wonkette fame (Keyes 2006), Heather Armstrong, aka Dooce (Economist 2006), and Markos Moulitsas Zúniga of the Daily Kos (Schulman 2007).

Bloggers' influence became evident when they began to change discourse in the mainstream media. As mentioned in Chapter 1, a much-cited case of blogosphere influence occurred in 2002 on the occasion of Strom Thurmond's 100th birthday celebration, in which Trent Lott made a reference to Thurmond's run for US President as a segregationist, suggesting that if we had followed Thurmond, the US would have had fewer problems (Nation 2002). Although this incident was broadcast live over C-Span, the mainstream media ignored the incident until the outcry generated through the blogosphere forced the issue into the conventional press (Bloom 2003).

Another incident first covered by bloggers before mainstream media was forced to take notice involves Dan Rather of *60 Minutes. On an episode of 60 Minutes,* Dan Rather showed documents that suggested that George W. Bush did not fulfill his service with the Texas Air National Guard adequately. Despite many newspapers repeating the *60 Minutes* allegations in their headlines, the legitimacy of these documents was almost immediately put into question by bloggers (Gibbs 2004). The bloggers noted that during 1972, typewriters could not have produced the alleged documents. The type setting and fonts that can so easily be produced today could not have been created by typewriters commonly used at this time. This incident not only led to the firing of several high-ranking individuals at *60 Minutes*, but also led to Dan Rather's early retirement from *60 Minutes* and the *CBS Evening News* (Economist 2004). Dan Rather had taken over anchoring the *CBS Evening News* from Walter Cronkite twenty-four years prior to this incident, and had inherited Cronkite's role as America's most trusted person. All this was lost as a result of the inaccurate reporting that was uncovered by bloggers.

We have discussed the origins of blogging, the influence of blogging, and the appeal of blogging. We will look at the elements that make up a blog and how one plans to start blogging next.

THE ANATOMY OF A BLOG

Figure 12.1 shows a typical blog entry for a hiking blog. Some of the common elements that comprise a blog can be seen here. Blogs typically have a title, header image, navigation (home and about), additional navigation to blog posts (not shown), a search feature, the

FIGURE 12.1 A typical blog entry
Source: Automattic Inc.

most recent blog post, a set of categories (not shown), and a set of widgets (not shown). Each blog post has a standard set of features available, such a title, date written, text of post, link for comments, and author (estiller). Blog posts also allow the embedding of links, images, and videos. Blog categories identify various topics that the blog addresses. For example, the hiking blog might include additional outdoor activities, such as kayaking, rock climbing, cross-country skiing, snowshoeing, and so on. This is because blog posts are geared to the author's experience, as opposed to being topic-driven. This allows readers to more easily find topics of interest.

There is a wide array of widgets that one may choose from, including a *blog roll,* meta-functions, a calendar identifying posts, categories, list of authors, connections to various social media, photo gallery/slide show, and many other features. The meta-functions allow blog authors to log in and administer their blogs by adding new posts or comments or changing the appearance of the blogs.

The blog roll widget has historical significance as an important means by which individuals found blogs of interest. Blog authors created a community of bloggers by listing each other in their blog rolls, so bloggers who appeal to another blogger appear in that person's blog roll. These mutual links would help elevate the popularity of those bloggers by sharing their pool of readers.

Now that we have established the fundamentals of blogging, the next topic discusses how to start one's own blog.

HOW TO CREATE YOUR OWN BLOG

There are a number of free options available for setting up a blog. Wordpress will be used to illustrate how to set up a blog in this chapter, because it is not only free to use, but is also open-source. As open-source software, Wordpress can be used and customized by other organizations to host their own blogging platform. For example, Plymouth State University uses this software to create a blogging facility for students, faculty, and staff.

Planning the Blog

When planning a blog, one should consider what contribution one can make to an already sizable blogosphere. Generally speaking, one should write not only about what one knows, but also about what might distinguish you from the millions of other bloggers. Finding locally or regionally specific topics could establish a means to attract an audience. For example, one could blog about life as a student at one's university, about local farm stands, about recipes that use ingredients primarily from locally sourced ingredients, local entertainment and recreational opportunities, about local artists, about local bands or other performers, about local sports teams, about local political issues and politicians, about how current events influence life in one's home town, about one's experience facing personal challenges, and so on.

As one plans blog content, the rules of netiquette should be recalled from Chapter Two. One should reflect positively on oneself by using correct grammar and spelling. Blogging facilities generally include a spell checker to assist in this matter. One should ensure that the content is accurate and disclose any conflicts of interest, such as political leanings (in the case of a political blog). One should also avoid perpetuating stereotypes. Because blogs include a comment feature, one should be mindful that passions can be aroused, and should not invite a harsh dialogue by using inflammatory language. For example, if one is a sports fan and blogging about the rival team using inflammatory language, this could invite an inappropriate comment from a fan of the rival team. This sort of harsh dialogue is known as *flaming, and should be avoided.*

Another issue that new bloggers should be aware of is spam. Many unscrupulous organizations attempt to leave software-generated comments at blogs. Most blogging tools have a means to prohibit these automated comments, like CAPTCHA. You may recall from Chapter Three that CAPTCHA asks people to interpret a distorted image of letters.

Creating the Blog

One can pay a fee or create a free blog. The main distinguishing features of a free blog versus a fee-based blog is advertising and the URL. The URL of a free blog always ends in *wordpress.com. The fee-based URL omits the "wordpress"* portion of the URL. Free blogs also may have advertising, whereas the fee-based blog does not. The possibility of advertisers posting an offensive message on your blog is worth considering. The need for advertising can be avoided if one's organization hosts its own version of the Wordpress software.

The following steps lead to the creation of a blog at the wordpress.com site. If your institution sponsors its own blog facility, the first two steps will differ, but the rest will likely apply.

1. Navigate to wordpress.com, and an invitation to create a blog will appear.
2. Provide the beginning portion of your blog URL. For example, the hiking blog uses "nhhikeblog" for this purpose. The URL nhhike.wordpress.com was already in use, so adding "blog" to the URL made it unique. So, the URL for the hiking blog is nhhikeblog.wordpress.com.
3. Once you have found a unique URL for your blog, a window like the one shown in Figure 12.2 opens. Enter your e-mail address, your user name, and a password. Make sure you make note of your password and user name, because these will be necessary to log in in order to make posts and administer your blog.

Get started with WordPress.com

E-MAIL ADDRESS

estiller@plymouth.edu

We'll send you an email to activate your account, so please triple-check that you've typed it correctly.

USERNAME

estiller

Your username should be a minimum of four characters and can only include lowercase letters and numbers.

PASSWORD

•••••••••   👁 Show

Great passwords use upper and lower case characters, numbers, and symbols like !"£$ %&.

🔑 Generate strong password

BLOG ADDRESS

NHhikingBlog   ✕   wordpress.com Free   ▼

Choose an address for your blog. You can change the WordPress.com address later. If you don't want a blog you can sign up for just a username.

FIGURE 12.2 **Getting started with Wordpress**
Source: Automattic Inc.

4. After your blog account has been created, you may customize your blog. When you select "My Sites," as shown in Figure 12.3, and then select "Settings" at the bottom left-hand side of the window, you may specify your blog's title and tag line. The title and tag line will both be prominently featured on your blog, as can be seen in Figure 12.5, so it is worthwhile to select these carefully. A series of other decisions can also be made using the settings window, such as if your blog should be indexed by search engines.

5. Adjust the look and feel of your blog by selecting "Themes and Customize," as shown in Figure 12.4. Select a theme for your blog by exploring the available themes. Keep in mind that some themes are for a fee, while others are free to use. Once a theme is selected, it may be customized by clicking on the customize link at the bottom of the theme.

6. You may customize themes by adding images to the header, as shown in Figure 12.5. Other customizations are also available, such as changing fonts and color schemes.

7. Select widgets for your blog by clicking on the widget menu item. Widgets can be selected on the menu side bar, as shown in Figure 12.5. They can also be accessed from the Wordpress dashboard from the "Appearance" menu item, as shown in Figure 12.6.

8. Once the blog is customized, the next step is to create posts. Blog posts can be created by selecting the "Posts" option on the dashboard sidebar, as shown in Figure 12.6.

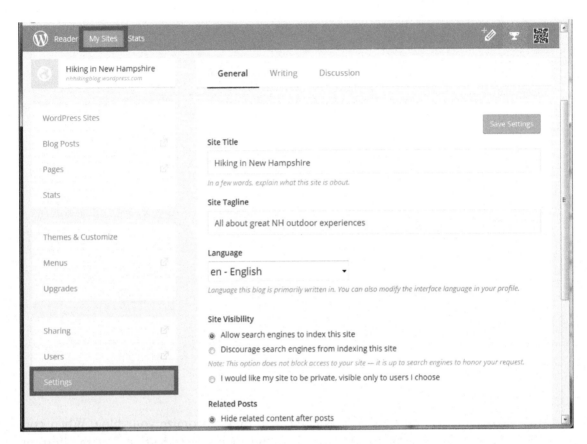

FIGURE 12.3 **Setting up your blog**
Source: Automattic Inc.

When one presses the "Add New" button, a window like the one shown in Figure 12.7 opens so that you can write your blog post.

9. Figure 12.7 shows a typical post. The text area contains the content of the post, which includes text, links, and an image. The links are shown in blue. The icons above the text area allow formatting of the content in addition to adding links, images, and other multimedia. To add a post, place your content in this area and format as desired.

10. Save your post frequently as a draft until you have completed your post. The "change status" option on the right-hand side of the window, shown in Figure 12.7, can be used to specify how your post should be saved: as a draft, as an immediate post, as a post pending review, or as a post to appear at a scheduled time and date. This status should be changed to draft until your post is ready to publish.

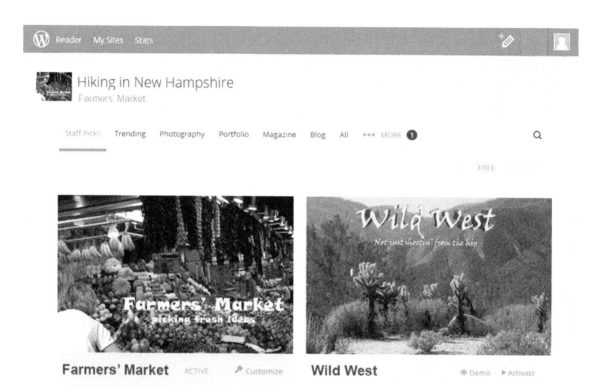

FIGURE 12.4 Selecting a theme for your blog
Source: Automattic Inc.

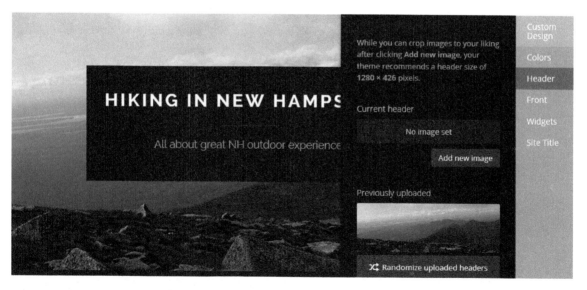

FIGURE 12.5 Customizing a theme
Source: Automattic Inc.

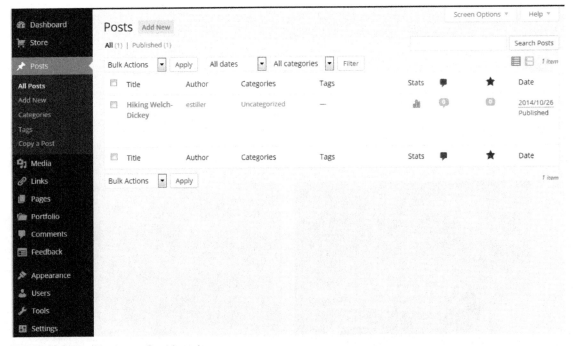

FIGURE 12.6 **The Wordpress Dashboard**
Source: Automattic Inc.

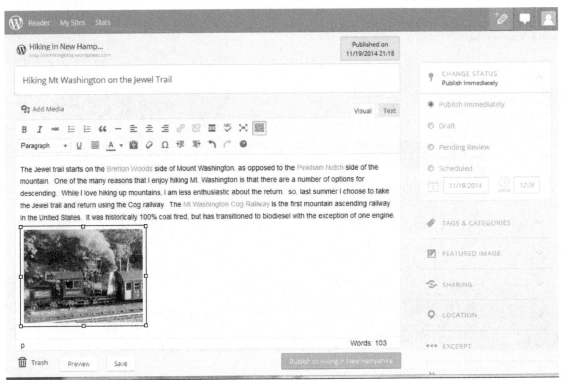

FIGURE 12.7 **Adding a Blog Post**
Source: Automattic Inc.

11. Format your post by using the provided icons above the text area. To determine what each icon can be used for, simply hover your cursor over the icon in question and explanatory text will appear.

12. Consider associating your blog post with a category. For example, the hiking blog could have a variety of categories, like hikes, snowshoes, cross-country skis, rock climbs, and so on.

13. When you are ready to publish your post, update the change status to "publish" and press the publish button located at the bottom right side of the text area.

You are now a blogger. Many find blogging to be a satisfying way to present their ideas to the world. Hopefully, you will as well.

SUMMARY

Blogs are specialized web sites that allow periodic entries, resulting in a chronological sequence of posts. Blogging became a popular means for individuals to express themselves when easy-to-use blogging tools became available. Certain bloggers took on the role of citizen journalists and have influenced content in the mainstream media. Others have used blogs to create an online journal, to share recipes, to provide technical how-to information, or to provide business advice or other information.

Blogging is an appealing activity for a number of reasons. People simply enjoy expressing their thoughts to an audience. Others seek to gain prominence as writers or for their novel perspectives or ideas. Blogs can be found during web searches, from references from other blogs, in blogging directories, or by word-of-mouth.

REFERENCES

Armstrong, H. "About." http://dooce.com/about/, 2014.

Bhuiyan, O. "Technorati-the World's Largest Blog Directory-is Gone." http://www.business2community.com/social-media/technorati-worlds-largest-blog-directory-gone-0915716 , June 16, 2014.

Blood, R. *The Weblog Handbook: Practical Advice on Creating and Maintaining your Blog.* Cambridge, MA: Perseus Publishing, 2002.

Bloom, J., "Blogosphere: How a Once-Humble Medium Came to Drive Elite." American Political Science Association 2003 Annual Meeting, Philadelphia, PA, 2003.

Cauley, L., "Internet speeds vary across USA, leaving a 'digital divide'." *USA Today*, 2009.

Davis, R. *The web of politics: The Internet's impact on the American political system*. New York: Oxford University Press, 1999.

Drummond, R. "About." http://thepioneerwoman.com/about/, 2014.

Economist. "Dropping the anchorman." *Economist*, 373(8403) (2004): 36.

Economist. "Going Pro." *Economist*, 381 (2006): 67–68.

Edsall, Thomas B., Faler, Brian (December 11, 2002). "Lott Remarks on Thurmond Echoed 1980 Words". *The Washington Post*. Retrieved May 26, 2010

Gibbs, N., Bacon Jr., P., Cooper, M., Dickerson, J. F., Duffy, M., Novak, V., & ... Bjerklie, D. (2004). BLUE TRUTH, RED TRUTH. (Cover story). *Time*, 164(13), 24–34.

Herring, S. C., I. Kouper, et al. (2004) Women and Children Last: The Discursive Construction of Weblogs. *Into the Blogosphere, Rhetoric, Community, and Culture of Weblogs*.

Keyes, C. (2006). Blogging. *Texas Monthly*. Austin, TX, Emmis Publishing. 34: 62–62.

Lenhart, A. and Fox, S. (2006). Bloggers, A portrait of the internet's new storytellers, PEW Internet and American Life Project.

McChesney, R. W., Scott, B. (2004). *Our Unfree Press: 100 Years of Radical Media Criticism*. New York, The New Press.

Nation (2002, December 30). Lott Should Resign. *Nation*. pp. 3–4.

Schulman, D. (2007). After crashing the gate of the political establishment, bloggers are looking more like the next gatekeepers. *Mother Jones*. San Francisco, CA, Foundation for National Progress. 32: 30–82.

Technorati (2008) State of the Blogosphere / 2008. Retrieved June 15, 2009 from http://technorati.com/blogging/state-of-the-blogosphere/

Zúñiga, H. G. D., E. Puig-I-Abril, et al. (2009). «Weblogs, traditional sources online and political participation: an assessment of how the internet is changing the political environment.» *New Media and Society* 11(4): 553–574

CPSIA information can be obtained at www.ICGtesting.com
Printed in the USA
LVOW02s1918020915

452592LV00002B/17/P